Shaker Built

Shaker Built

The Form and Function of Shaker Architecture

Paul Rocheleau and June Sprigg

Edited and Designed by David Larkin

The Monacelli Press

A DAVID LARKIN BOOK

First published in the United States of America in 1994 by
THE MONACELLI PRESS
10 East 92nd Street, New York, New York 10128

Library of Congress Catalog Card Number: 94-076580
ISBN: 1-885254-03-2

A DAVID LARKIN BOOK

Printed and bound in Italy

Contents

6 Introduction:
Dawn to Midday

12 The Builders

70 The Family

108 At Home

158 At Work

198 In Between

232 Twilight into Dawn:
The Loss and Renewed Life
of Shaker Buildings

272 Acknowledgments

Introduction

When I was younger, I built a house. Oh, I didn't pick up hammer and nails, but I wrote the checks and watched as carpenters, electrician, and plumber turned the ideas in my head and the blue lines on architect's paper into a beautiful little timber-frame house, full of light and air and places for the cats to curl up in. Children loved my little home, set among maples on a hillside that sloped down to a miniature brook. By the grace of serendipity, the skylight over the bed admitted the face of the moon whenever it waxed and grew full.

I learned a great deal about everything as I planned and built my house. I learned the difference between vision and reality, as well as the necessity for both. All my best imagining of a finished roof and walls could not keep the rain from my head when the building existed merely as a post-and-beam frame. All my best guesses about the view from the windows could not reveal the sight of branches and sun before the windows were paid for and installed.

I learned more than I thought possible about money—where it came from, what I had to do to earn it, and what the relation was between my work and the balance of my life. I learned much, much more than I really wanted to, about thrift, and how to consider the cost of a cup of coffee before I spent the money for it, when the roof still needed shingles. (To this day, alas, I am still recovering from my inevitable reaction to the rigid requirements of enforced thrift.) I learned what it was like as a woman in her thirties on her own to hire and oversee an all-male construction crew. We all learned and we all benefited.

I learned how valuable to the animal and human spirit are shelter and "home." I learned how fiercely I would fight to protect what is mine. I learned how a house could be a haven or a prison, how it could keep people out of my life as well as invite them in. I learned that a home, for me, is female, a "she." I learned that a fresh, new home does not have ghosts. I learned that I could do anything I wanted to do, but that I had to choose with care what it was exactly that I wanted. I learned that there is no such thing as "security," no matter how many homeowners' insurance bills I paid, and that in spite of my relative safety from hurricane, tornado, earthquake, flood, lava flow, geyser eruption, and meteor strike, my beloved home was still vulnerable to fire, wind, and thieves. I learned that in spite of all this, it was entirely likely that my house would long outlast me. I learned that someday, someone else—in fact, probably a long series of someone elses—would call *my* house "home." I learned that my home, which I shaped, in turn shaped me (a reality that Winston Churchill had expressed in so many words earlier in our century).

In the end, the most valuable thing I learned was that I could let my house go. When my life changed, and I outgrew at last my need for a one-woman incubator, I put my house on the market and sold it within a few months. Some friends could not believe I could part with the house I had worked so hard to create. But others, who knew me best, understood that I could leave it because it was no longer useful to me, and that there would in time be another house that was more useful to my growing and changing life. And so it has proved.

Anyone who has built or bought or simply inhabited a home or building for business will understand what I am talking about, and will similarly comprehend the significance of the world that the Shakers built on American ground in the eighteenth, nineteenth, and twentieth centuries. Beginning with a dream of the Society's founder, Englishwoman "Mother Ann" Lee, a way of life gradually took shape that involved the commitment of thousands of believers and the energy of many thousands more who spent time as Shakers but did not ultimately give the whole of their lives.

In 1774, Mother Ann landed in New York with a handful of followers, preaching the creation of a new order of human life "more like angels than men" who modeled themselves closely after the pattern established in word and deed by Christ. To this end, celibacy and charity (including the complete sharing of resources in a communal economy) were keystones of Shaker life.

After her death ten years later, the growing number of converts established their first large-scale communal living group in 1787 in New Lebanon in upstate New York, on the

border of the Berkshire hills in Massachusetts. At that time, the Shakers believed it was necessary for them to separate from "the World," a term that the Shakers used as Jesus used it when he advised the apostles how to continue his work and carry the gospel after the impending crucifixion. As missionaries traveled from New Lebanon, which was to remain the Shaker Society's spiritual center throughout the nineteenth century, other groups of converts in New England eventually established their own settlements, patterned after New Lebanon. The original community was guided by what was understood to be divine instruction from God to the Parent Ministry of two women and two men who made their principal home at New Lebanon.

In the first decade of the 1800s, more new communities were established by missionaries in what was then the American West, in Ohio and Kentucky. New Lebanon supplied the male and female leaders for each of the new villages as it gathered into order.

By about 1820, the Shakers were very well known as something absolutely novel in the New World (or Old). While their celibacy and communal life caught the attention of observers, it was their practice of dancing in worship that really startled outsiders. Until the fourth quarter of the nineteenth century, when the number of Shakers had declined enough so that they no longer represented a threat to their neighbors and

townspeople in the World, the publicity that the Shakers got was bemused at best, and more often critical, in terms of everything except the quality of their workmanship and their honesty in business. Their plain, unadorned style in all things from buildings and furniture to clothing frequently earned the ridicule or contempt of others.

Much has been made in our own century of the simplicity of Shaker design, although now the reaction of the World tends toward admiration rather than disapproval. This simplicity is not to be confused with carelessness or crudeness. The rule of thumb for Shaker creations, whether a barn, basket, or sacred song, seems to have been something like this: If it is not useful or necessary, free yourself from imagining that you need to make it. If it is useful and necessary, free yourself from imagining that you need to enhance it by adding what is not an integral part of its usefulness or necessity. And finally: If it is both useful and necessary, and you can recognize and eliminate what is not essential, then go ahead and make it as beautifully as you can.

Those rules of visible creation were consistently applied to architecture. The first generation of converts, who came into the Society in the years immediately after the American Revolution and who were responsible for building shelter, workshops, and barns for their newly assembled communal families, drew on what they had learned about construction and design from their experience in the World.

Most of the earliest Shaker buildings no longer survive, since many were dismantled, moved, or substantially altered by the Shakers themselves before 1850. The exception are the meetinghouses, the first examples of anything that can be called Shaker design, built in the late 1780s and 1790s in the communities in New York and New England. Even so, these buildings of worship were not regarded as sacrosanct when their usefulness faded. After the construction of large, convenient meeting rooms in communal family dwellings built or extensively renovated in the 1830s and thereafter, the old meetinghouses were frequently used for other purposes—in one case, as a workshop where garden seeds raised for sale on a commercial scale were sorted.

The Shakers' attitude towards their buildings was no more sentimental than their attitude about their own flesh-and-blood bodies. It was the spirit or usefulness within that mattered, not the vessel itself. If the building lost one use, it was converted to suit another. When the body grew frail and eventually died, the spirit simply moved on to another level of reality, one in which material bodies were not needed or useful.

The appearance of things—including buildings—mattered in the Shaker world, but not in the same way that it generally mattered in the World. According to the way the Shakers viewed life in general, looks counted for much, much less than substance. Physical homeliness was perhaps less of a handicap in the Shaker world than anywhere else, because the beauty of the spirit was what was deemed important. The question of usefulness determined the worth of a tool, a chair, a building, or a person. Form resulted from function. The placement of settlements, buildings within a settlement, rooms within a building, and windows, closets, and other features within a room all derived from usefulness. In the Shaker world, the appearance of a thing or a person mattered only to the extent that it revealed the underlying function. Whatever did not interfere with function, served function. This is different from saying that whatever did not serve function, interfered with function. The former approach allowed Shaker craftsmen and craftswomen a remarkable degree of freedom within what at first glance seem very stringent restrictions.

In its way, the concept known to the Japanese as *ma* (loosely translated as "the space between" objects) was a key part of the Shaker-built landscape, whether in a room or between the communal family settlements. Knowing how to place the useful component was as much a part of Shaker design as knowing what to leave out. The restrictions on creativity as properly obeyed by a faithful, devoted Shaker gave rise to a characteristic genius for proportion and sensitive placement of the parts of the whole.

Within days after I sold and left my house, I traveled to Japan to accompany an exhibition of Shaker design sent to a museum in Tokyo. While there, I had the chance to visit Kyoto, where I went to see the Zen garden at the temple of Ryoan-ji. This is the famous dry garden of fifteen rocks placed in a sea of raked gravel.

In the essay I wrote for the exhibition catalog, I likened the Shakers' gift for knowing what to leave out to that of the priest/gardener who had created the garden at Ryoan-ji, and I compared the clarity and openness I perceived in my Shaker friends to what I thought was the absolute openness of that Zen garden.

It was a fitting ending, and beginning, to learn something I had not known about Ryoan-ji—one of the fifteen rocks is always hidden from any ordinary human vantage point on the ground. What had seemed to be the epitome of utter revelation proved instead to be the ultimate sleight-of-hand, completely concealing what it seemed to reveal.

In the course of assembling this book, Paul Rocheleau and I concluded that Shaker architecture is like the rocks at Ryoan-ji. We invite you to explore his look at some of the best of what remains of what the Shakers built.

The Builders

Because the Shaker Society chose after 1787 to live apart from "the World" for the sake of their spiritual convictions, new converts generally settled on farms that belonged to some of the earliest members in their area. At first, communal families of up to a hundred people packed themselves into the houses given by the original landowners. At Hancock, Massachusetts, for example, one Sister recalled sleeping fourteen to a room when the Church Family was formally "gathered into order" in 1790.

As soon as possible, however, men who came into the faith with building skills began to add barns, workshops, an office and store, and dwellings to their settlements. Early journals record a steady flurry of expansion, with a new building of some kind typically going up every year, in a program of construction that continues to impress observers with its ambition and energy.

Understandably, some of the earliest efforts were less successful, depending on the training and abilities of the first ingathering of converts. In 1858 at New Lebanon, New York, Brother Isaac Newton Youngs, writing his communal family's recollections of the "Manner of Building," noted that the founding members "were poorly qualified for building" because they were struggling to make a living on their mountainside farmland, they did not have much experience, because they needed to expand their crowded facilities in a hurry, and they did not have much money for materials. As a result, the earliest buildings there were constructed "for the present, on a small scale, and in a cheap style," until the community had sufficient time, skill, and resources to build more permanently.

What is remarkable is how quickly the New Lebanon and other Shaker communal families improved their holdings and properties. By the early nineteenth century, a new crop of boys raised by the Brothers were being trained in the building trades, and in time the workforce combined old-timers with experience learned in the World with young men who got all their training in-house. Shaker communities loaned their most skilled builders back and forth to assist with each others' planning and construction

when the need arose. For example, Brothers James Daniels and Elijah Brown were sent from Canterbury, New Hampshire, to the Shaker community at Harvard, Massachusetts, to help frame and raise a building in 1810. When the Canterbury Church Family was planning its new Office and Store, constructed in 1831, they sent Brothers to Hancock's Church Family to tour the brand-new 1830-31 brick dwelling for ideas and technical input. The Canterbury Office and the Hancock Dwelling share features like roof skylights in the attic.

By the early nineteenth century, builders in many cases had begun to lavish time and care on construction details. When the North Family Dwelling at New Lebanon was dismantled in the early 1970s, workers were impressed at discovering features including baseboards dovetailed around a chimney, mortise-and-tenon joints at the top corners of interior and exterior door surrounds, or architraves, and splined joints between sheathing boards underneath the siding to make the building airtight. They found marks on construction dating to around 1818 from a circular saw, a very new piece of equipment in rural America at that time.

At times the Brothers with experience in the building trades— including carpentry, timber framing, stone and brick masonry, shingle-splitting, plumbing, and blacksmithing—joined forces with hired professionals when it was practical to do so. At Hancock and New Lebanon, for example, records show that the community hired stonemasons to build foundations, stone walls for fields, and even the Round Stone Barn. Other communal families hired carpenters on occasion.

The remarkable output of the builders is all the more impressive when it is considered in the context of the Brothers' other responsibilities, primarily farming in summer and woodcutting for fuel and lumber in winter. The advantages of a communal economy were apparent. There were enough men so that some could devote themselves to building, and the income from the sale of manufactures, typically managed by the best business heads in each communal family, grew into considerable savings within a few decades, especially because the Shaker Society frowned on buying on credit and thus kept free from the burden of interest payments.

Relatively little is known today about the sources of ideas and specific buildings or designs that undoubtedly gave Shaker builders the foundation onto which they added the special needs of their communal society—practical considerations like large size and spiritual requirements including simplicity, separation of the sexes, careful construction to reflect working for the glory of God, and a passion for the type of efficiency that improved the quality and comfort of the workers' lives. For example, the loss of records at Hancock's Church Family means that we know next to nothing about the sources of inspiration for the 1826 Round Stone Barn, one of the earliest if not *the* earliest round barn in North America.

However, it makes sense that the most gifted builders borrowed what they observed in the World, primarily large, well-built urban structures like schools, asylums, hospitals, public buildings, and churches, and then adapted what they liked for their own uses. It would be reasonable to assume that the builders were given access to builders' design books and other plans published in periodicals. For communities whose records survive, notably the Church Family at New Lebanon, an extensive, detailed record of the building processes is available, although the journals are characteristically mute on the sources of design.

We know more about the source of building materials. Builders prepared what they could at home, from sawing stone to building brick yards, and also bought what they needed, including (perhaps surprisingly, from our vantage point) timber, most of which had been quickly felled for building, firewood, and clearing land for fields and pasture. Account books record many purchases, particularly of glass, which the Shakers did not find practical in the least to make. Since the typical community owned some two or three thousand acres or more by the mid-nineteenth century, many communal families had access to their own quarries, clay pits, gravel beds, and woodlots. The Hancock Shakers had a small iron mine. When the Shakers in Kentucky built with stone, they used limestone; the Shakers in New Hampshire used granite, and the Hancock Shakers used marble. Kentucky carpenters used a lot of white walnut, Hancock carpenters worked with butternut, and the New Hampshire Shakers favored birch and maple, although workers in every village used dozens of varieties of wood available.

East View, of the Brick House, Church Family Harvork

The Shaker community at Pleasant Hill, Kentucky, began its existence in 1805, when three missionaries sent from the Shaker "capital" at New Lebanon, New York, made converts of the farm family who owned land nearby. By 1823 the community had grown into five large communal families and a number of smaller satellite groups with a total population of just under five hundred, making it one of the largest Shaker villages in America.

This view, taken from the outlying communal family called the North Lot, shows the Centre Family's vast stone dwelling at the far right and the East Family Dwelling and work buildings on the left.

West of the Centre Family at Pleasant Hill, Kentucky, more
converts gathered on land owned by Elisha Thomas, who "set
out in the Gospel" in mid-August 1805. In 1818, the West
Family became an aged members' order. The Old Stone Shop,
built in 1811-12, and the brick West Family Dwelling, 1821-22,
line up precisely along the main east/west road that linked the
West, Centre, and East Families.

following page
View of the Church Family, Hancock,
Massachusetts, from the southwest, showing Laundry and
Machine Shop, circa 1790s; Dwelling, 1830-31; Sisters' Dairy
and Weave Shop, circa 1795-1820; small brick Ministry Wash
House, circa mid-nineteenth century; Poultry House, 1878;
and Round Stone Barn, 1826-64.

left

The Centre Family Dwelling at Pleasant Hill, Kentucky, 1824-34, retains its original dark blue paint. The baseboards are dark red.

The color choice is puzzling because Shakers in the eastern communities obeyed rules believed to have been received by divine inspiration in the mid-nineteenth century to reserve blue paint for the interior woodwork of the meetinghouse alone. Many Shakers in the New York and New England communities considered the Kentucky Shaker villages, a thousand miles distant from the Society's spiritual center at New Lebanon, New York, a little too removed as well from some of the guidelines that all Shakers were expected to follow.

above

Brothers and Sisters ascended separate, side-by-side stairs in the Centre Family Dwelling at Pleasant Hill, Kentucky, begun in 1824 and completed ten years later. The woodwork retains its original dark blue and red paint. A wrought iron spindle at the turn of the banister, painted and shaped to be indistinguishable from its ordinary wooden mates, has given quiet, unwavering strength to the handrail for more than a century and a half.

Original paints and stains reveal that Shaker interiors were meant to be colorful. The Centre Family Dwelling built between 1822 and 1833 at South Union, Kentucky, retained its bright ocher-yellow and orange-red color on the woodwork, now revealed by the removal of later coats of paint. This is the Sisters' door to the meeting room on the first floor, looking through to their stairs beyond.

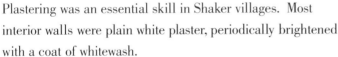

Plastering was an essential skill in Shaker villages. Most interior walls were plain white plaster, periodically brightened with a coat of whitewash.

A patch of plaster awaiting repair in a back corner of the cellar of the Centre Family Dwelling at South Union, Kentucky, begun in 1822, reveals the roughly scored scratch coat, or underbase, made of earth mixed with hair.

The rectangular hole was intentionally created to accommodate a nailer, or wooden "brick," to which the chair rail was eventually fastened.

In 1830, the Church Family at Hancock, Massachusetts, began their fine new dwelling to house nearly a hundred members in greater comfort in a six-story building with nearly 37,000 square feet of living and storage space.

The Family's Elder, William Deming, headed the project and assisted in the building, including mason and joiner work. In an 1832 letter to a fellow Elder, he detailed the work, including sawing 565 feet of blue limestone for the basement story on the south side (shown) and laying 350,000 bricks. "We commenced our building," he concluded, "and in ten weeks from the placing of the first stone in the cellar the house was neatly laid up and the roof put on...The work is all well done. There is none to excel it in this country." The bricks were finished with four coats of a thin red paint so that the white mortar did not show. The shutters (since replaced) and doors were painted green, probably the bright grass green favored before 1860. When Sister Hannah Cohoon of Hancock painted her now-famous Tree of Life in 1854, she used the same striking contrast of orange-red and bright green, perhaps influenced by the color scheme of her Shaker home.

Most Shaker villages built some buildings in brick, which was durable and fire-resistant. Some communities had their own brickyards.

These bricks and the wooden mold are from South Union, Kentucky. The mold, one of hundreds that were once in use, was packed with wet clay, then removed so the brick could be fired in the kiln. The indentation, called a frog, in the length of the brick, formed by the raised part of the mold, would fill with mortar and provide a strong bond. These may be among the earliest bricks made in America to use this feature.

These are among the earliest Shaker bricks known. Brother Isaac Whyte, whose name was scrawled with a flourish in the wet clay, never to be seen if the brick were used, died in 1814.

All that remains of the Meetinghouse that the Shakers built in 1818 in South Union, Kentucky, is the carved limestone lintel with date that once topped the center window on the second floor. The Meetinghouse, which faced the Centre Family Dwelling begun in 1822, was razed around 1830, after the Shakers sold the property.

The top of the 1818 Meetinghouse lintel reveals a message left by the unknown stonecutter that remained concealed throughout the building's life and was brought to light again only when the building was destroyed. This detail is in Hebrew.

Shaker builders seemed to be fond of commemorating their construction efforts with carved or painted date stones. The front door to the cattle level of the Round Stone Barn built by the Church Family at Hancock, Massachusetts, boldly proclaims its 1826 date of construction.

1811 date stone, Old Stone Shop, Pleasant Hill, Kentucky.

A spiritual preference for freedom from adornment did not allow Shaker builders to indulge in "superfluous" ornament. But Shaker buildings inside and out reveal the makers' virtuosity and what can be perceived as a creator's delight in shaping details with a lavish devotion of time and obvious care. Shaker "simplicity," like the simplicity of traditional Japanese design, is probably best understood as freedom from fussiness, not disregard for quality or appearance.

On the Centre Family Dwelling at South Union, Kentucky, begun in 1822 and finished in 1833, the limestone lintels and sills are neatly grooved. The work was done by six Brothers, headed by principal stonemasons Jesse McCombs and Urban E. Johns. One of the Brothers, David Barnett, was African-American. The Shakers in Kentucky, as elsewhere in the Society, were pacifists and apolitical but opposed the institution of slavery on spiritual and moral grounds.

Detail of drainpipe and limestone cornice and gutter, Centre Family Dwelling, 1822-33, South Union, Kentucky.

Detail of stone windowsills and doorsills, Smoke and Milk House, 1835, South Union, Kentucky.

Shaker buildings, stylistically removed from American architecture because the Shakers turned their backs on changing fashions as useless and wasteful, were nevertheless recognizable as "cousins" in construction and basic style to more mainstream products of the same time and place.

Shaker buildings in the Northeast were shaped by Yankee New England and New York Dutch regional traditions. Shaker buildings in Kentucky and Ohio were shaped by a dual influence: the Southern regional building traditions overlaid by the Northeastern Shaker tradition of New Lebanon, New York, the spiritual center of the nation's Shaker Society, where the buildings were regarded as models for Shaker builders everywhere.

The blending of the two influences is visible in the Centre Family Dwelling at South Union, Kentucky, begun in 1822 and completed in 1833. The overall plan looks like large Shaker communal dwellings back East, but the configuration of the chimneys and the shape of the back stair ell look more Southern.

The copper-lined limestone gutters on the Centre Family Dwelling, 1822-33, at South Union, Kentucky, were an initially high investment in labor and cost that paid off well over time because they have never needed replacement.

The Centre Family eventually replaced the original white oak roof shingles with standing-seam metal roofing to eliminate problems caused by humidity.

above

This granite quarry was purchased around 1830 by the Church Family Shakers at Enfield, New Hampshire, and may have been the source of the building stone for their 1837 Dwelling, a landmark stone construction effort. The massive building has more than thirty rooms on seven floors and measures a hundred by fifty-eight feet.

A large granite block remains where it was cut from the living rock at the quarry because it did not split straight. The drill holes are visible in the section to the right.

The Shakers who built in stone seemed to prefer the
uniformity and neatness of cut or sawn stone to the
irregularity of fieldstone, in spite of the additional labor
and cost.

This is the limestone Forge or Blacksmith's Shop built in 1846
by the Center Family Shakers at Mount Lebanon, New York.

The Machine Shop built by the Church Family Shakers at Enfield, New Hampshire, in 1849, combines sawn granite corner quoins and window surrounds with fieldstone walls, a relatively uncommon method in Shaker architecture. The building originally had three stories.

In 1837 the Church Family at Enfield, New Hampshire, planned and began work on an enormous new seven-story granite dwelling, one of the largest structures constructed by the Shaker Society. Shaker records credit the design to Ammi Burnham Young, a local non-Shaker architect whose other New England buildings include Dartmouth Hall at nearby Dartmouth College and the Vermont State House in Montpelier. The Shakers hired Luther Kingsley and a team of twenty-four stonemasons from Boston, who completed the work in six months.

The cellar has cooking facilities, stone bakeovens, and food-storage rooms in addition to massive brick and stone arches that run the length of the building to support its weight. The main kitchen was in the center of the first floor, flanked by waiting rooms for the Sisters and Brothers. Above the dining room on the second floor is the large meeting room, with retiring rooms and small storage rooms on either side. The third and fourth floors hold eight retiring rooms each, twenty feet square, with storage rooms between every two rooms. The fifth and sixth floors were for storage, with a crawl-space attic above topped by a bell tower which commands a fine view of the surroundings.

The "bones" of Shaker structures, even brick buildings, were timbers in post-and-beam construction. The timbers were hewn by hand from tree trunks with broadaxes or sawn into shape at the mill. Preparing the timbers took months of work. Assembling the parts could take place in a day, if the building were small.

On raising day, crews of timber framers hoisted the heavy beams and fitted the carved tenons into their mortise holes, like assembling a giant's building set.

In the Centre Family Dwelling at South Union, Kentucky, begun in 1822 and finished in 1833, the main attic over the ell shows the type of post-and-beam construction called a king post.

The original 1854 timber-frame construction in the attic of the Wash House, built by the North Family Shakers at Mount Lebanon, New York, was added to in the 1870s, when grain bins were built under the eaves. A chute in the attic led down to a small grinding mill on the second floor. The arrangement was probably added at the request of Elder Frederick Evans, a progressive social and dietary reformer who was so adamant about the superiority of whole-grain bread that he carried his own loaves on a proselytizing trip to England.

This marvelous machine for boring holes in timbers is extraordinary in design and workmanship in comparison with similar devices made by mechanics in "the World." It bears the stamped initials RW and the date 1851. The owner acquired it near New Lebanon, New York, within a mile of the Shaker village. It is attributed to Brother Richard Woodrow, a member of the Center Family. He left the Shakers in 1853, just two years after making this implement.

This machine, used to drill holes, superseded the hand-turned augers shown nearby.

Timber framers used augers to drill holes into beams so that they could use chisels to cut out the mortise, or to drill holes for inserting the large wooden pins that hold post-and-beam building frames together.

Detail of boring machine.

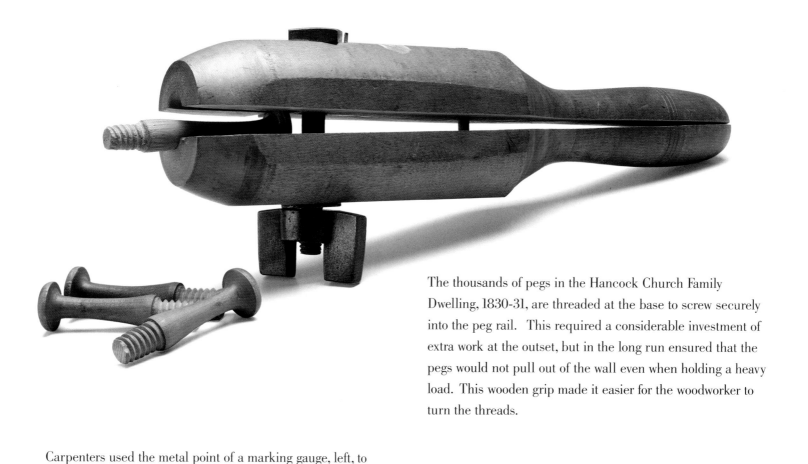

The thousands of pegs in the Hancock Church Family Dwelling, 1830-31, are threaded at the base to screw securely into the peg rail. This required a considerable investment of extra work at the outset, but in the long run ensured that the pegs would not pull out of the wall even when holding a heavy load. This wooden grip made it easier for the woodworker to turn the threads.

Carpenters used the metal point of a marking gauge, left, to scribe lines indicating the width of clapboards or the placement of mortises. The chalk line, right, contains a string covered with powdered chalk, snapped along a beam to mark lines for hewing or sawing timbers. Most nineteenth-century chalk lines were messy open spools; this Shaker version keeps the chalk neatly inside a box.

The huge mallet, called a beetle or commander, was used to pound the mortise-and-tenon joints of timbers into place. The smaller mallets were used to drive the wooden pins that secured those joints or to pound chisels in finish carpentry.

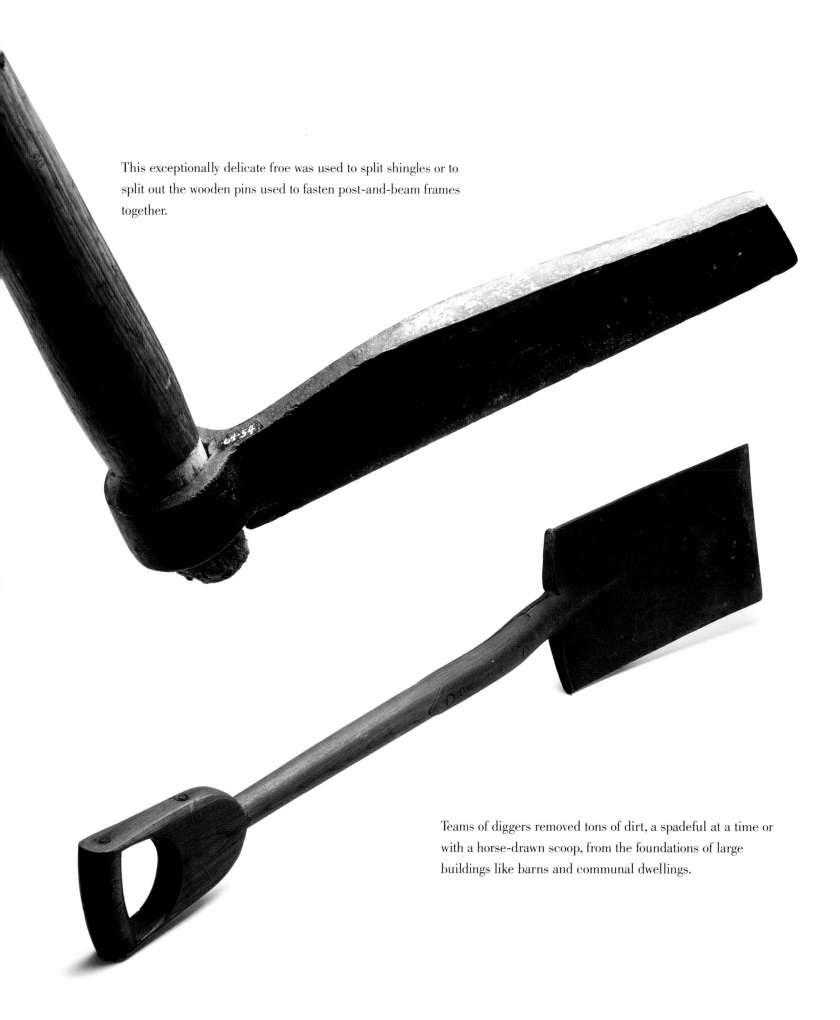

This exceptionally delicate froe was used to split shingles or to split out the wooden pins used to fasten post-and-beam frames together.

Teams of diggers removed tons of dirt, a spadeful at a time or with a horse-drawn scoop, from the foundations of large buildings like barns and communal dwellings.

This fine, Shaker-made plumb level, mounted originally on a pointed "Jacob's staff," was used to sight foundations and walls.

Brother Robert Johns (1795-1863) was the principal carpenter of the splendid Centre Family Dwelling at South Union, Kentucky. Two of his planes rest atop a panel from a South Union cupboard. Shaker woodworkers like Brother Robert typically provided the communal family with buildings, furniture, coffins, and other wooden items as needed.

Very fine handmade Shaker planes do exist, but the workers were often provided with purchased tools because it was usually more practical to buy them than to make them. The top plane is stamped *1/RJ/1836 and N.H. STOUT/W.W. Rickey/Louis[vill]e, Ky.* The foreground plane is stamped *R JOHNS/1824.* An 1817 penny serves as a washer. Although individual Shakers were not supposed to mark the tools they used as their own, Brother Robert was not the only worker known to lay claim in this way to a particular set of tools.

1893

A blacksmith forged large wrought-iron numerals for an unidentified building in the Shaker community at Union Village, Ohio.

Shaker builders bought tools but sometimes also made their own. These very fine planes are attributed to Brother James Daniels, an early convert to the Church Family at Canterbury, New Hampshire, in the 1790s. The planes, made between about 1800 and 1830, are for (clockwise from top): rabbeting, coping, sash, molding, and panel raising.

left
Shaker planes from Canterbury, New Hampshire, on a twelve-foot Shaker workbench from New Lebanon, New York, in the woodworking shop at Hancock Shaker Village in Massachusetts.

Bow saws were used for cutting curves. Straight cuts were made with a regular handsaw.

right
One of the last steps in building was painting or staining the interior woodwork. In the early and middle nineteenth century, the Shakers favored a thin, translucent stain that allowed the grain of the wood to show. These pigments, part of a rare collection, were used by the Shakers in Canterbury, New Hampshire.

44

The Church Family Office at Harvard, built in the 1840s, preserves some of the finest interior Shaker woodwork in existence with its original finish. In this first-floor room, built-in storage units flank a door to a closet. Stairs on the other side of the wall, at a right angle to the built-ins, descend to the cellar. The placement of the cupboards to the right of the closet door reflects the angle of the stairs.

right
Some of the finest Shaker wrought-iron door hardware remains in the midsize dwelling built in the early to mid-nineteenth century by the South Family at Mount Lebanon, New York. This example is in the communal family's meeting room, built on the second floor above the dining room.

Wrought-iron door latch, Church Family Dwelling, 1830-31, Hancock, Massachusetts.

Shaker builders in Kentucky liked arches, which were seldom seen in the New York and New England communities. On the second floor of the Centre Family Dwelling at Pleasant Hill, Kentucky, looking from a Brothers' retiring room on the east to a similar room for Sisters across the hall, arched openings alternate with ordinary doors. The building was begun in 1824 and finished a decade later.

Brothers' door on east side, Centre Family Dwelling, 1824-34, Pleasant Hill, Kentucky.

preceding page

Kentucky Shaker builders favored high ceilings, practical because they made for cooler rooms in steamy southern summers, and the use of the arch. Shaker builders in New England and New York made lower ceilings, which conserved warmth in cold winters, and did not incorporate arches. This is the second-floor hall in the ell of the Centre Family Dwelling, 1822-33, at South Union, Kentucky.

Builders throughout the Shaker network incorporated transoms and sidelights to "stretch" daylight into halls.

Shaker builders used more turned work than most of their worldly neighbors. For the new brick dwelling built in 1830-31 by the Church Family at Hancock, Massachusetts, for example, Brothers skilled at the lathe turned hundreds of spindles for the Brothers' and Sisters' stairs, drawer pulls for 369 built-in drawers, knobs for 245 built-in cupboard doors, thumb screws for more than a hundred windows, and thousands of pegs for peg rail on all six stories.

Some of the finest work in the entire six-story Church Family Dwelling at Hancock, Massachusetts, was made for the topmost floor, the upper level of a two-story attic, an area that was off the beaten path. A pair of handrails rise to carved newel posts.

above
Top of newel post, attic stair rail, Church Family
Dwelling, 1830-31, Hancock, Massachusetts.

Stair rail, attic of Church Family Dwelling.

56

Arch, second-floor hall, Centre Family Dwelling, South Union, Kentucky.

Shaker builders spent more time remodeling, renovating, and even moving older buildings than constructing new ones. As the needs of the growing communal families changed, existing buildings often shifted functions and were remodeled as necessary.

This stone building at Pleasant Hill, Kentucky, was the first permanent structure in the village. When it was built in 1809, it housed the Ministry and the small Centre Family. In 1812, the Ministry moved to their own shop, where they slept and worked. (After 1821, when they moved to a new Ministry Shop, the 1812 structure eventually served as a farm workshop, schoolhouse, and housing for hired hands.)

Meanwhile, the old 1809 stone shop served in turn as a tavern for travelers and as a shop where the Farm Deacons slept and worked.

right

In some work structures Shaker builders seemed to pay more attention to placing windows where they made sense on the interior than concerning themselves with a symmetrical exterior wall. The former Dry House at Canterbury, New Hampshire, served as an apple-drying facility in the nineteenth century and was converted to a woodworking shop in the early twentieth century, when the Dry House was connected to the Church Family's Laundry.

Although white paint was at first reserved for the meetinghouse alone, according to a long series of "divinely inspired" rules written in the 1840s, the community at Canterbury, New Hampshire, like other Shaker villages in the Northeast, painted all its formerly colored buildings white in the later nineteenth century. The Church Family buildings at Canterbury resemble other small New England villages in "the World" around.

In the 1840s the Church Family at Harvard, Massachusetts, built a very large Office. Several construction features, including the design and construction of doors and built-in drawers, help identify furniture made by the same group of Shaker Brothers at Harvard. The Office, which has about forty rooms, is preserved as a private residence.

The recessed front door of the Office built in the 1840s by the Church Family at Harvard, Massachusetts, a relatively unusual feature in Shaker buildings, provides a practical shield against rain or snow for those fumbling with a key at the door.

The door configuration, with the horizontal panel on the top, is a typical detail of American building in the Federal period in the early nineteenth century. However, it is not common in surviving Shaker architecture. It appears on other doors in buildings, on built-in cupboards, and on freestanding furniture made by Brothers at Harvard.

Looking down the west stairs from the second-floor
landing, Trustees' Office, 1839-41, Pleasant Hill, Kentucky.

following page
The large brick Trustees' Office at Pleasant Hill, Kentucky, begun in 1839 and finished in 1841, was a milestone in Shaker architectural accomplishment. At its heart, dual freestanding staircases ascend three floors to a skylit landing in a graceful *pas de deux.* The building was designed by self-taught Brother Micajah Burnett. Most large Shaker buildings had separate, side-by-side stairs for the celibate Sisters and Brothers. Here, where visitors from "the World" did business, lodged, and dined, men and women were expected to observe the same rules of separation.

Both sets of stairs begin with curved steps on the first floor.

following page Domed oval skylit cupola at top of spiral stairs, third floor of Trustees' Office, 1839-41, Pleasant Hill, Kentucky.

The attics of large Shaker dwellings are characteristically as well planned, built, and finished as the more visible rooms below. Attics were used primarily for storing off-season clothing, carried up and down in spring and fall.

The third-floor attic of the Centre Family Dwelling, 1824-34, at Pleasant Hill, Kentucky, has built-in poplar drawers and a dormer that serves as a skylight to brighten the space and help reduce the risk of fire from a candle or lantern.

In the early to middle nineteenth century, work buildings were customarily painted light colors like yellow or tan if they were near the road and darker colors like red or brown if they set back.

The Bee House was built by the Church Family Shakers at Canterbury, New Hampshire, in 1837 for use as a dry house for curing lumber. In 1865, it became the beekeeper's storage area, and in 1940, was moved to its present location near the site of the main barn to serve as a milk house.

The Family

Life in the Shaker world was defined by a dynamic tension. The sexes were always together, in a large communal family living under one roof—and always apart, since celibacy was a cornerstone of the Shaker way. Like the ancient Chinese principles of *yin* and *yang*, Shaker men and women circled each other in their homes, workshops, and meetinghouses in a never-ending, side-by-side dance, always joined and always separate. The dual principles of communication and separation pervaded their everyday lives and did much to shape Shaker architecture.

The basic economic and emotional living unit in the Shaker world—where a Shaker would have said that he or she "belonged"— was the communal family, which ordinarily occupied a single dwelling surrounded by work buildings for its own enterprises, including barns, an office and store, mills, separate work buildings for Sisters and Brothers, and a mass of small support buildings including privies, woodsheds, and ash houses (for storing wood ash to make lye for soap and other purposes.) Communal families ranged in size from a dozen to about a hundred people.

In each village, there were usually three basic types of "orders:" a Novitiate, or gathering, Order, where most incoming would-be converts were required to stay for a sufficient period of time to determine whether the match was suitable from both the convert's and the community's point of view; a Junior, or intermediate, Order, where unmarried or single would-be converts lived; and a Senior, or Church, Order, where fully committed converts resided, having decided to live their lives as faithful Shakers and having freely given all their property to the community for everyone's benefit.

Communal family life afforded very little opportunity for solitude or privacy, at least physically. Spiritually and emotionally, individuals were given time and encouragement to focus their energy on inward-turning meditation and prayer. The usual arrangement was that a group of four to six or more members of the same sex shared a sleeping room, dormitory-style. Everyone was ordinarily expected to rise and retire at the same time. Room assignments were usually made by the communal family's two Elders and two Eldresses, who served as loving fathers and mothers to the "children of God the Father and Mother" in their care. Since the Shakers believed that ties of kinship and marriage between individuals fostered selfishness (and ultimately the worldly evils of nationalism and war), they encouraged "universal love" and discouraged "particular friendships," not only between women and men, but also between members of the same sex. Cliques and the inevitable dissension of what the Shakers called the party spirit, as in divisive political parties, were seen as threatening to the tremendously important quality of "union" that was the Shaker communal family's ideal. To this end, roommates were regularly cycled into new rooms in the dwelling house and new relationships, as well as into new jobs in new work areas with new work partners. Several evenings a week, small groups of Sisters crossed the hall onto the Brothers' side, taking their chairs with them, and met for what were called union meetings, social gatherings devised early in Shaker history to promote appropriate brotherly and sisterly relations instead of unwelcome private love relationships. A few surviving letters show that the partner groups of male and female roommates enjoyed affectionate and mutually beneficial relationships, helping each other with tasks belonging to the men's or the women's side.

Up to a hundred members of each communal family gathered at least three times daily in their dwelling's dining hall. On some evenings, everyone assembled again for worship in the dwelling's large meeting room. Since the sexes were strictly divided in both large rooms, and met all together, it was probably the norm for most individuals to recognize each other mainly at a distance and to perhaps be more like acquaintances or neighbors than intimate friends.

On Sunday, when the weather permitted, the communal family gathered at the meetinghouse to worship. At times, the entire society of three to as many as eight communal families, with from two hundred to five hundred members, might congregate for a special service. As part of their spiritual discipline, individuals met privately with their Elder or Eldress at intervals to confess their sins or shortcomings and to receive guidance for growing well and whole in spirit, mind, and body.

The Shakers sought to re-create a human society that was, in their words, born of a "spiritual" rather than a "natural" order—that is, they sought to enter into a new covenant with each other, not as husband and wife and father and mother, but as innocent, separate, celibate "children" living in the family of Christ. In Shaker life, the old ties dissolved, and formerly married couples became Brother and Sister, as did former sons and daughters and fathers and mothers.

Did the system work perfectly? Of course not. It took a special kind of person to accept the rules of Shaker life, and research is showing that far more people tried and eventually left the Shaker life than remained through the end of their days. There were men and women who fell in love and left together, either publicly and honorably or by running off at night; there were individuals who up and left, sometimes to the communal family's delight and sometimes to distress and sadness; there were parents who in the end could not bear to lose their own family ties and who departed with their children; there were "bad fish caught in the gospel net" who lost the battle to mental illness, criminal behavior, or alcoholism and left in disgrace. The ones who remained were mostly the ones who fit—people who above all else were able to consistently place their own self-interest second to that of the group. The Shakers themselves recognized that theirs was not a life for everyone, and they smiled at the outsider's frequent concern that someday "the whole world might become Shaker" and in so doing sign the human species' death warrant.

Church Family buildings, Hancock, Massachusetts.

In 1794, the Church Family at Sabbathday Lake, Maine, built its gambrel-roofed Meetinghouse under the direction of timber-framer Brother Moses Johnson, sent by the Ministry at New Lebanon, New York, to oversee the design and construction of Shaker places of worship. The Sabbathday Lake meetinghouse is in the opinion of many the finest extant example of a Shaker meetinghouse, reverently preserved in the least altered condition.

Today, members of this community—America's sole communal family of Shakers at this time—continue to gather for worship in the Meetinghouse when weather permits; otherwise, they assemble in the meeting room of the Church Family Dwelling. Marching in worship ceased at Sabbathday Lake in 1907 in favor of a service that retained the song, prayer, Bible reference, and shared testimony of earlier public meetings.

left

Afternoon sunlight pours through western windows in the Meetinghouse built in 1824 at Mount Lebanon, New York. Each of these enormous windows has fifty-five panes. The Church Family gathered to worship on Sunday afternoons after public services in the morning, customarily conducted by leaders of the North Family, a Novitiate Order. When members of New Lebanon's seven other communal families assembled in the Meetinghouse, they generally congregated by Order— Novitiates with Novitiates, Senior Order with Senior Order, and so on.

following page

Inside the first floor of the Meetinghouse built in 1794 by the Church Family Shakers at Sabbathday Lake, Maine, benches for Brothers and male visitors on the South continue to face seating for Sisters and female visitors on the North. The Meetinghouse retains its handsome early coat of dark blue paint on the interior woodwork.

left

The only time that the members of all the village's communal family living groups ordinarily met in one spot was when they assembled to worship in the village's one meetinghouse. Up to three hundred or more Shakers could get glimpses of each other at these times. In most Shaker villages, the community's buildings grew around the meetinghouse, often the first joint venture, built at the heart of the original settlement, called the Church Family (or Centre Family in Kentucky and Ohio). A fence customarily separated the meetinghouse from the road that led to "the World" and even from other, nonsacred Shaker dwellings and work buildings.

The large Meetinghouse at Pleasant Hill, Kentucky, faces the Centre Family Dwelling. Sisters and Brothers crossed the main road on separate, side-by-side walks, entered through their own doors, and sat on their own sides, women on the west and men on the east. The Meetinghouse was built in 1820.

above

In 1824, the Church Family at Mount Lebanon, New York, moved their original gambrel-roofed meetinghouse and on its site erected a new barrel-roofed meetinghouse that astonished Shakers and outsiders alike with its size and innovative construction. It was the largest interior space for miles around.

This view is of the north side. The building housed a vast first-floor meeting room, more than 78 feet long and 63 feet wide, with a 25-foot ceiling. It is one of the largest Shaker meetinghouses and the only one built with an arched roof, which, like the earlier gambrel roofs, made it structurally possible to build a very large room without the need for interior supports so that several hundred Shakers could freely join in the dance worship.

The Meetinghouse at Canterbury, New Hampshire, built in 1792, is unusual because it does not sit right on the main road through the village, as many other Shaker meetinghouses do. Rather, it sits in quiet solitude at the southernmost edge of the village, separated from the rest of the buildings in the communal Church Family by a picket fence, and even more clearly separated from "the World" by a long, grassy lane.

The Canterbury meetinghouse was one of a group of nearly identical gambrel-roofed structures framed by Brother Moses Johnson, sent in the 1780s and 1790s from the center of Shaker spiritual life at New Lebanon, New York, to build meetinghouses according to the "pattern at the Mount," the original meetinghouse of this style at New Lebanon, built in 1785.

Maples planted by Shaker children in the late nineteenth century have grown to venerable old age in the lane in front of the Meetinghouse, built in 1792 at Canterbury, New Hampshire.

following page
Visitors to the Shaker community at Canterbury, New Hampshire, approached the oldest part of the village, the Church Family, from the south up a long hill. The oldest building is the gambrel-roofed Meetinghouse, built in 1792, at the right. Behind it is the Church Family Dwelling, begun in 1793 and extensively remodeled over the next two hundred years. The Church Family Shakers were in time joined by Second and North Families further up the road.

Shakers from other villages liked to call Canterbury the City on the Hill, after a biblical reference to a celestial settlement.

The entire communal family gathered regularly in a large meeting room in the dwelling for worship or family business. Centre Family Brothers at Pleasant Hill, Kentucky, in chairs or benches brought to the east side, faced the ranks of Sisters who sat on the west. If the meeting included the sacred dance, the seats were moved to clear the floor for rows of Shakers who were taught to step together in precise order.

following page
The Centre Family's meeting room, with its distinctive domed vault ceiling, is on the second floor of the building's large ell to the rear.

85

Shaker dwellings typically included a large room for communal family meetings. At South Union, Kentucky, the Centre Family's meeting room was located on the first floor of the ell on their dwelling, built between 1822 and 1833.

When the building was new, the communal family of seventy celibate Sisters and Brothers filed quietly down separate, side-by-side stairs and through separate, side-by-side doors into the meeting room. The Sisters' side was on the west. Communal families met together at home in evening worship at least once a week.

The clock was originally purchased and used in the Trustees' Office. Old photographs show a large wall clock in the niche.

right
Morning light illuminates the east or Brothers' side of the meeting room in the Centre Family Dwelling, 1822-33, at South Union, Kentucky. The built-in cupboard was probably used to store Bibles and hymnals between meetings.

88

Elder William Deming, the principal designer and builder of the Church Family Dwelling begun in 1830 at Hancock, Massachusetts, described the building's 100 large doors, 245 cupboard doors, 369 built-in drawers, and 95 windows with a total of 3,194 panes of glass. Records reveal that Brother Comstock Betts made the doors; details of construction on the drawers have made it possible to identify their probable makers, Hancock Ministry Elders Grove Wright and Thomas Damon. The woodwork, originally stained bright yellow and orange, was refinished later in the nineteenth or early twentieth century by the Shakers.

The Shakers, who loved light both metaphorically and literally, asked their builders to flood their homes and work buildings with daylight. The passage from the north into the meeting room on the second floor of the Centre Family Dwelling, 1824- 34, at Pleasant Hill, Kentucky, is brightened by a tall arched transom. Morning sun highlights the Brothers' side of the large room where the communal family met to worship.

In worship meetings the Shakers sat on light, easily portable benches that they moved out of the way when they rose to join together in the sacred dance. This bench, made about 1830 in Enfield, New Hampshire, is in the meeting room of the Church Family Dwelling, 1830-31, at Hancock, Massachusetts.

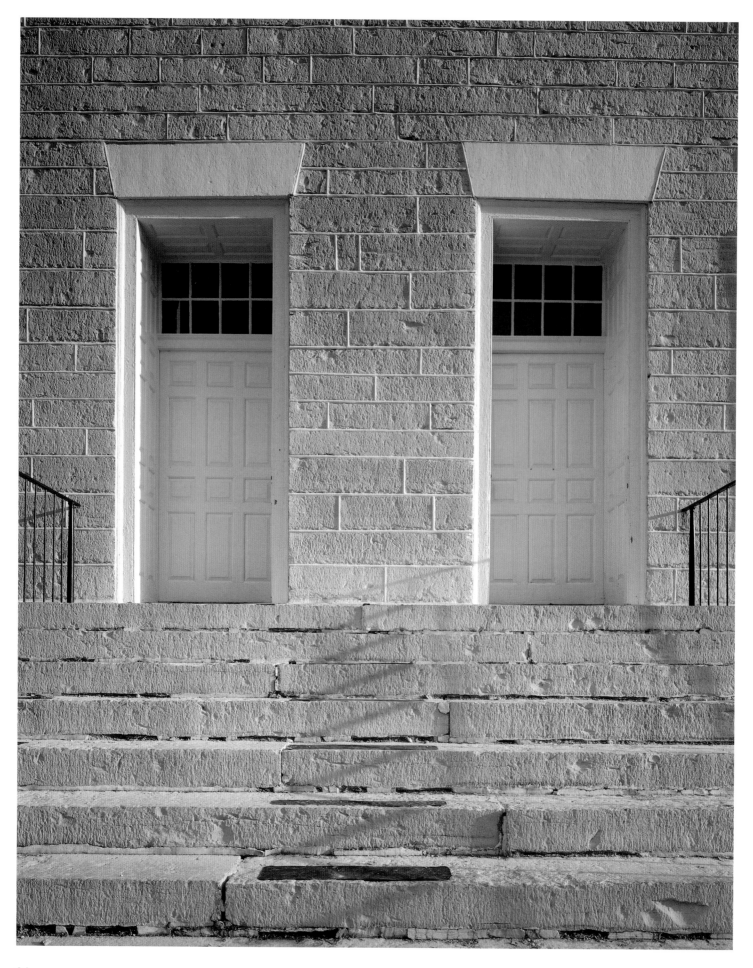

left

Shaker life was defined by the Society's remarkable combination of communalism's inescapable togetherness and celibacy's enforced separation. Large Shaker buildings, especially dwellings shared by women and men, were characterized by separate, side-by-side doors, which unequivocally announced the Shakers' distinctive manner of living to "the World" passing by.

Throughout the dwelling behind the split facade, an invisible but uncrossable line divided the residence into virtually identical, mirroring halves—a Sisters' side on the west and a Brothers' side on the east. Women crossed the line into the Brothers' rooms for housekeeping and for "union meetings," social gatherings of assigned across-the-hall male and female roommates several evenings a week after supper.

above

Two doors side by side are standard in Shaker buildings. But the doors in the ell of the Centre Family Dwelling at Pleasant Hill, Kentucky, are conspicuous as an unexpected trio.

The reason for three doors is practical, not spiritual or philosophical, as is the case with the double doors to separate women and men. The left door opens to stairs to the infirmary rooms on the second floor, the right goes into one of two bake rooms behind the large kitchen, and the door in the middle enters the kitchen.

95

Sisters' passage into the meeting room from the south,
Centre Family Dwelling, 1824-34, Pleasant Hill, Kentucky.

Morning sun reflected from the shining clean floor gathers
along the arched ceiling corner of the meeting room in the
Centre Family Dwelling, 1824-34, at Pleasant Hill, Kentucky.

Members of the communal family met privately with the Elder
or Eldress to confess shortcomings and receive spiritual
guidance. This retiring room is on the second floor
Brothers' side of the Centre Family Dwelling, 1822-33, at
South Union, Kentucky.

The door to the retiring rooms in the ell on the second floor of
the Centre Family Dwelling at South Union, Kentucky, opens
to the side-by-side stairs for the celibate Brothers and Sisters
who shared this residence.

The second-floor hall of the ell on the Centre Family Dwelling, built from 1822 to 1833 at South Union, Kentucky, divides the Sisters' retiring rooms or bedrooms on the west from the Brothers' rooms on the east.

This level has twelve "retiring rooms" or bedrooms. There are ten similar retiring rooms on the first floor below, and two more on the attic story above.

Separate, side-by-side stairs for Sisters and Brothers rise from the first to the third floors in the Centre Family Dwelling, 1824-34, at Pleasant Hill, Kentucky.

The ceilings in Kentucky Shaker buildings were built high—in this case, twelve feet high—to help keep the rooms cooler in the steamy southern summers.

following page
A door to a second-floor retiring room on the east side for Centre Family Brothers, left, faces a door to its partner Sisters' retiring room. Male and female roommates from such pairs of rooms met in the Brothers' room in friendly "union meetings" several evenings a week to socialize in a way that fostered brotherly and sisterly affection, not romantic attraction.

preceding page

At Hancock, Massachusetts, the Church Family divided their 1830 dwelling into celibate men's and women's quarters separated by an exceptionally wide hall. The Sisters slept dormitory-style on the west side of this second floor and the floor above, facing the Brothers' identical rooms on the east. (Other Shaker communal families chose instead to house the sexes in wings separated by the stairs.)

The large meeting room on the floor below was designed to be divided on occasion into separate rooms for the Sisters and Brothers by means of two sliding partitions that dropped into the room from this level. At the far end of the hall, the six small doors at the peg-rail level open to the space between the walls where the partitions were stored when raised and not in use. The partitions no longer exist, but the pulleys and lead weights that hoisted them remain in the upper floors.

Built-in cupboard over drawers on the Sisters' side of the meeting room, Church Family Dwelling, 1830-31, Hancock, Massachusetts; looking into room 6.

At Home

The dormitory-style dwelling house was the great heart of the buildings that clustered in the communal family's settlement. From here the dozen or hundred members emerged every morning to go to work, to here they returned at noon for dinner, repeating the outflow in the afternoon and influx back for evening supper, worship or social meetings, and sleep. The dwelling was "home."

Although both men and women shared the dwelling equally, it seems to have been the particular province of the Sisterhood, much in the same way that the barns were the Brothers' territory, and much in the same way that American women ruled the roost inside the house and men were kings of the farmyard. The Brothers do not seem to have entered the Sisters' side, while the women regularly went into the men's rooms to clean and change linens. When the small groups of women and men met in the evening for

"union meetings," during which they talked, sang, and enjoyed each others' company in an approved fashion, it was the Sisters who took their chairs across the hall to the Brothers' rooms, not vice versa. In addition, the kitchen and food-storage rooms in the cellar were the domain of the Sisters, as was the attic, where off-season clothing was stored.

In light of all this, it seems reasonable to suppose that Shaker women had a lot more to do with the design and construction of Shaker dwelling houses than might at first be assumed, in spite of the fact that the actual labor was done by the Brothers. Since women were responsible for cleaning the house (while men cleaned the barn!), the characteristic spareness of the interiors and myriad details that reduce the effort required to tidy as many as forty rooms on a regular basis seem inspired by the requests and suggestions of the Sisterhood.

There were at one time at least seventy Shaker dwelling houses in more than twenty principal communities from Maine to Indiana to Florida. While the largest are among the glories of surviving Shaker architecture, not all dwellings were created equal. Each reflected the personality of the group that built it, which had of course a life of its own

as the unique product of a dozen to a hundred individual personalities melded by the Shaker pursuit of "union," or collective harmony. Some, like the magnificent Centre Family Dwelling at Pleasant Hill, Kentucky, were landmarks, stately structures of five or six stories and forty or fifty rooms, solid testimony in stone, wood, and plaster to the abundance and material and spiritual success of the Shaker communal family by the early to middle nineteenth century. Some were quite small and much more modest, although their builders would certainly be encouraged to build them as well as possible in the characteristic Shaker way. Everything depended mainly on the size of the communal family and its relative prosperity, which was usually directly tied to the quality of the farmland it owned and the manufacturing and marketing acumen of its workers and business agents or Trustees, who were responsible for selling the community's products for income. Some communal families, more prosperous than others, built in stone or brick rather than wood. Some were more progressive, always ready and willing to tear down an older structure and build anew, while others were more conservative, preferring to renovate and expand rather than to abandon the old. There is evidence of subtle human rivalries between the communal families in one village and between the villages as well. The Church Family Shakers at New Lebanon, New York, tacked a handsome, spacious new addition to their original 1788 dwelling in 1831-32, just a year after the Church Family Shakers at Hancock, Massachusetts— about five miles down the road—replaced their cramped earlier quarters with the fine new Brick Dwelling. The Centre Family at South Union, Kentucky, began work on their handsome new dwelling in 1822. By the time they had raised the walls and set the date stone in 1824, the Centre Family of Kentucky's other Shaker community at Pleasant Hill had begun work on *their* new dwelling, which was larger than the one at South Union.

Whatever their particular size and details of construction, the dwelling houses shared a number of features, and Shakers who were permitted to travel between villages admired each others' unique variations on a theme even while feeling remarkably at home. The ground floor or basement level generally housed the kitchen and food-storage cellars, taking advantage of the natural coolness underground and placing the kitchen where cooking was warmer in winter and cooler in summer, and where the noise and smells of food preparation might be two floors removed from the sleeping rooms.

For obvious reasons, the dining room was customarily adjacent to the kitchen, as often as not on the first floor above as in the basement. The kitchen and dining room conveniently accommodated interior supports like columns, but the meeting room was ordinarily designed structurally so the space was uninterrupted by columns that would have interfered with the neat lines and circles of the Shakers' dance worship. The upper floors were where members slept in "retiring" rooms, and above all the rest, a characteristically large and pleasantly light attic formed the crown.

Some communal family members who lived apart from the dwelling stayed in the Nurse Shops and other workshops. Others who lived separated from the communal family in the dwelling were the Trustees, women and men who lived and worked in the Office and Store, handling all the family's business concerns; the Caretakers, two men who lived in a separate house with the boys, and their two female counterparts who took care of the girls in another small house; and the two men and two women in the Ministry, the highest spiritual authority in the bishopric, which consisted of two or three villages in geographical proximity, usually within one state. In early Shaker history the Ministry lived on the upper floors of the meetinghouse, then moved to larger, more comfortable quarters in separate Ministry Shops by the early to middle nineteenth century.

In 1830-31, the Church Family at Hancock, Massachusetts, erected a splendid six-story dwelling with nearly 37,000 square feet of living and storage space. The principal designer and builder was Elder William Deming, who described his communal family's accomplishment in 1832 with understandable pride and pleasure. The new dwelling, home to nearly a hundred members, was made of 350,000 bricks at a cost of only $8,000 for hired labor. Elder William wrote, "The work is all well done. There is none to excel it in this country...The whole work has been performed in the space of nineteen months...Now Elder Benjamin I think by the time you have read all my broken scrawl you will think our purse is pretty empty, which in truth is the case. But as we have [given] in obedience to our good Mother Ann's words—So we expect to receive. Her precious words were these, 'Your hands to work and your hearts to God and a blessing will attend you.' This we have found true."

Church Family Dwelling, 1830-31, Hancock, Massachusetts, from the south.

following page
The Centre Family at South Union, Kentucky, began work on its handsome new dwelling in 1822, set the 1824 date stone when the walls were raised and the roof was built, and moved in 1833, seventy strong, into its forty-two rooms (not counting closets).

Like most large Shaker dwellings, it has a symmetrical facade and plenty of windows, including dormers in the attic. The placement of windows made visual sense from both outside and inside. The facade is unusual for having a single door rather than the standard double front doors so that celibate Sisters and Brothers could enter separately but simultaneously, side by side (although stone steps ascend to the door from each side).

The South Union Centre Family Dwelling was a fine example of the glory days of Shaker building, when communities bursting with prosperity and optimism could not imagine a time when their Society would not need spacious quarters, built to last a long, long time, for ever-increasing numbers of converts.

113

Front of first-floor hall, Centre Family Dwelling, South
Union, Kentucky.

Front of second-floor hall, Centre Family Dwelling,
South Union, Kentucky.

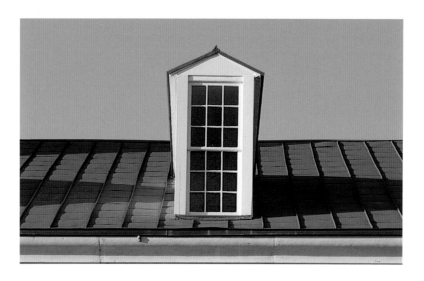

Central dormer in front of attic, Centre Family
Dwelling, South Union, Kentucky.

A morning view of the Brothers' side of the Centre Family Dwelling at South Union, Kentucky, shows the vast size of a dormitory-style residence for a large Shaker communal family that numbered seventy when the building was new. The Dwelling, begun in 1822 and finished eleven years later, has forty-two rooms on four floors. Visitors likened large Shaker dwellings to college buildings, prisons, hospitals, and other examples of institutional architecture designed to house a large number of people.

The Shaker communal family ate and slept here, but spent most of the day at work in dozens of other surrounding buildings.

Like monasteries and convents throughout the world and over time, the communal Shaker family rose, ate, met, prayed, and retired in unison to the sound of a bell.

The Centre Family at South Union, Kentucky, built an unusual bell tower that perched airily on the roof and was not accessible through an ordinary stair tower. During one fire emergency, a Brother had to clamber out along the roof's peak to strike the bell by hand—four stories aboveground—because the fire had burned through the rope! This replica was reconstructed according to historic photographs of the original.

The builders of the North Lot Dwelling at Pleasant Hill, Kentucky, used clapboard, shingle, stone, and brick.

Would-be Shakers first lived in the "gathering," or Novitiate Order, where they were asked to try the Shaker way of life before seeking full admission to the Society.

The North Lot Dwelling at Pleasant Hill, Kentucky, was built in 1815 and expanded in 1816 to house such potential converts. It is typical of small Shaker communal dwellings— large enough compared to ordinary households in "the World," but very small by Shaker standards.

The external chimney and its profile reminded Shaker visitors from New York and New England that they were in the South, where regional architectural traditions joined with Shaker building requirements to form an approach to Shaker building distinctive to Kentucky.

When their fine limestone dwelling was completed in 1834, the Centre Family at Pleasant Hill, Kentucky, nearly a hundred strong, moved into their new home. It was one of the largest and grandest of all Shaker dwellings. Like most Shaker communal dwellings, this one has retiring rooms or dormitory-style sleeping quarters on several floors; a large dining hall; a small, separate dining room for the two women and two men in the Ministry; a meeting room where the communal family assembled to worship or meet; rooms for an infirmary; a cellar with a kitchen and food-storage rooms; and an attic for off-season clothing storage.

The rooms on the Sisters' side reflect the light of the setting sun.

By the 1830s and 1840s, many of the Shaker families who could afford to do so built magnificent large residences in the belief that they would need sturdy dwellings to receive a steady influx of converts for the millennium that had already begun.

Smaller or less prosperous Shaker families chose to build more
modest dwellings in wood or brick. Brick was preferred in
part because it reduced the danger of a total loss by fire.

The West Family at Pleasant Hill, Kentucky, erected their
midsize dwelling in 1821 to house a group of around seventy-
five aged members, who worked at tasks that suited their years.

The Second Family of Shakers at Mount Lebanon, New York, built a stone workshop in the early nineteenth century. To the right is a very large frame workshop that housed the community's important chair-making enterprise during its development from the 1850s to 1863, when the South Family took over the business and became the major producer. Later, when the South Family dwindled in numbers, the chair enterprise reverted to the Second Family, and in the twentieth century this was the last chair factory at Mount Lebanon.

The Centre Family Dwelling begun in 1824 was a milestone in
the Shaker building tradition. The facade belies the immensity
of the limestone building's proportions. Its four stories rise
forty-six feet and span sixty feet from east to west. More than
forty rooms stretch this front section of the Dwelling and an
ell behind to 140 feet. The side-by-side front doors for
Brothers and Sisters are ten feet in height from the threshold
to the top of the transom window. The second-floor windows
are each seven feet tall.

The building impressed Shaker and worldly visitors alike when
it was completed after ten years of construction. The walls,
erected in 1825, were covered and "some work done" in 1826-27.
Upheavals in the community in the late 1820s contributed
to delays in construction.

Sisters' side of the Centre Family Dwelling, 1824-34,
Pleasant Hill, Kentucky, at sundown.

The Church Family at Canterbury, New Hampshire, built a
dwelling in 1793 and then continued to expand and remodel it
while Shakers continued to live there until the death of the last
Canterbury Shaker, Sister Ethel Hudson, in 1992.

This view from the northeast shows the ell added in 1837 to
house the communal family's large new meeting room on the
first floor, with new rooms for the New Hampshire Ministry,
above. On the third floor is a splendid attic with a half dozen
walk-in closets and more than a hundred built-in drawers.
The addition to the left was added in 1813 to provide additional
space for the Sisters.

Dormer window in Church Family Syrup Shop,
Canterbury, New Hampshire, where medicinal syrups
were distilled.

In 1883, the Church Family at Sabbathday Lake, Maine, began construction on a large, handsome brick dwelling to replace their old 1795 home, moved from the same site by a large team of oxen. At Thanksgiving in 1884, the Church Family sat down to their first meal in their new home. The small white portico is a nod to the style of the late nineteenth century. Records indicate that the building was designed by Francis Fassett of Portland, Maine, and that the contractor was George Brock, also of Portland.

Today, the Shakers at Sabbathday Lake continue to sleep, dine, and meet for worship in this Dwelling. This view shows a corner of the Ministry's Shop on the left and the 1794 Meetinghouse on the right.

The second and third floors of the Church Family Dwelling,
built 1830-31 at Hancock, Massachusetts, had twenty sizable
"retiring" rooms, or bedrooms, for a communal family of
nearly a hundred when the building was new. The Brothers
slept in the ten rooms on the east side of the building, with a
wide hall separating them from the Sisters' sleeping rooms on
the west side.

This retiring room, furnished as part of the museum
installation operated by Hancock Shaker Village, a nonprofit
corporation dedicated to preserving and interpreting Shaker
culture, shows typical retiring-room furnishings and Brothers'
clothing. The room's four or five occupants had little more
than beds and chairs, typically streamlined and free of
applied ornament so they were easy to move and clean.

right

The built-in cupboards and drawers in the 1830 dwelling were
the pride and joy of the Church Family builders at Hancock,
Massachusetts. Residents used step stools to reach the upper
drawers and shelves.

This unit is in a first-floor room near the main door on the
Sisters' side that may have housed the communal family's two
Eldresses. The topmost narrow cupboard, with its original
lock and bone escutcheon, was probably used for safekeeping
of important papers and communally owned valuables.

Members of the communal family traditionally dined together three times a day in silence, as much to avoid the roar of a hundred voices in a room unsoftened by curtains and carpets as to maintain a reverent spirit while receiving the blessing of food for the body. Sisters and Brothers ate together but sat on opposite sides of the room.

In the Centre Family Dwelling at Pleasant Hill, Kentucky, built between 1824 and 1834, the Sisters sat on the west side and took four-week turns cooking for and serving the Brothers and Sisters alike. The small built-in corner cupboard has a twin on the Brothers' side.

left
Room 6, Church Family Dwelling, Hancock, Massachusetts.

Sisters and Brothers ate meals together but sat on opposite sides of the communal dining room. They dined in silence for practical as well as spiritual reasons—the chatter of nearly a hundred voices is deafening in a room of plain plaster walls and pine floors. Windows on the inner wall to the left admitted daylight into the stairwells to the kitchen below. The large transom over the doors carried light into the first floor hall.

Dining Room, Church Family Dwelling, Hancock, Massachusetts.

140

The attic rooms on the front of the Centre Family Dwelling, built 1822-33 at South Union, Kentucky, are typically finished. The bar between the posts has holes for pegs from which clothing was hung.

The builders of the Church Family Dwelling, 1830-31, at Hancock, Massachusetts, joined six interior chimney flues into three external chimneys by bringing them together just under roof level on the sixth and topmost floor. Like other large Shaker dwellings, this one required flues for woodstoves in almost every room, between thirty and forty altogether. These flues converge in the attic's south room.

The attic rooms retain their original plaster, which lead builder Elder William Deming praised: "The plaster is covered with a coat of hard finish & is a beautiful white."

143

The eight inside rooms on the lower level of the two-story attic of the Church Family Dwelling at Hancock, Massachusetts, built 1830-31, are lit by natural light even though they do not have windows to the outside.

Windows on interior walls of these under-eaves rooms "stretch" daylight through one storage room into another. In two such rooms, a skylight brings additional light through the ceiling from a second, exterior skylight in the roof directly overhead on the topmost floor.

The ceiling racks with iron hooks were for storage of off-season clothing. The short door leads into a crawl space under the eaves that runs the length of the hundred-foot-long building.

right
Lower of double skylights into attic storage room, Church Family Dwelling, 1830-31, Hancock, Massachusetts.

144

Looking through interior window in attic
storage room to window on southern exterior wall, Church
Family Dwelling, 1830-31, Hancock, Massachusetts.

following page

A freestanding flight of stairs rises to the sixth and top floor
of the Church Family Dwelling at Hancock, Massachusetts,
built in 1830. Large, communal Shaker dwelling houses had
spacious attics, primarily for storage of off-season clothing.
Like the attics of most Shaker dwellings, Hancock's is airy and
thoughtfully planned, with skylights and windows on interior
walls to stretch daylight into inner rooms. The built-in cupboards
and drawers are typically made of local woods, pine and
butternut with cherry drawer pulls.

Dormer window from attic of Centre Family Dwelling, 1824-34, Pleasant Hill, Kentucky.

The attic stairs lead to a glazed door in a vaulted dormer that opens onto the roof, where those so inclined could enjoy the view commanded by the walkway protected by a balustrade. The dormer's placement makes visual and spatial sense from inside the building while disrupting the otherwise symmetrical facade by its slightly off-center position.

left

The attics of large Shaker buildings were typically as well designed and finished as any of the more public rooms below. The attic of the Church Family Dwelling, 1830-31, at Hancock, Massachusetts, is remarkable for its two stories, linked by a freestanding flight of stairs. Brass hardware on the steps once held rods that secured a long, woven carpet that protected the wood. The uppermost floor is brightened by skylights. Two large banks of built-in butternut and pine drawers flank the central staircase. The woodwork retains its original light orange wash.

The meetinghouses framed under the direction of Brother Moses Johnson are nearly identical, but different builders varied the placement of the stairs to the upper floors, where the Ministry lived and worked.

At Canterbury, New Hampshire, the two women and two men of the Ministry ascended steep stairs in an ell at the rear of the meetinghouse. In other communities, including Sabbathday Lake, Maine, the stair ell was placed to the side of the building.

The woodwork in Shaker meetinghouses was uniformly painted blue in the late 1790s or early 1800s. In 1878, progressive Elder Henry Blinn repainted the Canterbury meetinghouse in a lighter shade of blue, which remains in good condition.

right

In 1848, the New Hampshire Ministry moved from the second and third floors of the Meetinghouse into a more spacious, comfortable Ministry Workshop built just behind the Meetinghouse to the east.

This view shows a one-room ell at the back of the Ministry Shop, in 1854 originally "fitted up for a wood workman," probably Ministry Elder Joseph Johnson. The 1792 Meetinghouse is behind to the west.

In 1839 the Church Family at Sabbathday Lake, Maine, built a workshop and residence for the two women and two men in the Maine Ministry. The female leaders occupied the second floor, over the male leaders on the first floor. The shop was more comfortable and convenient than their previous quarters in the upper floors of the Meetinghouse. In 1875, the Church Family enlarged and improved this Ministry Shop. The large two-over-two windowpanes replaced the earlier windows in 1910.

The two women and two men who served in the Ministry as the highest authorities of several communities in one bishopric, or region, lived and worked apart from the communal families in small buildings designated for their use. Ministry Eldresses and Elders were ordinarily highly respected members of the community who could be trusted to guide their flocks wisely and live faithfully as two men and two women under a single roof. Separation from the communal family helped to promote objectivity and judiciousness in case of resolving disputes. The Ministry were expected to work with their hands like common members as well as to oversee the spiritual welfare of the villages in their care.

At Pleasant Hill, Kentucky, the men and women of the Ministry entered their workshop through separate, side-by-side doors. This building, erected around 1812, was called the Old Ministry Shop when a newer and larger workshop was built for the Ministry near the new Meetinghouse in 1821.

Only a handful of Shakers in any one village did not live with
the rest of their large communal family. The Brothers and
Sisters who served as the business managers for their
communal family, called Trustees or sometimes Office
Deacons and Deaconesses, ate, slept, and worked in the
family's office and store building.

The very large Trustees' Office at Pleasant Hill, Kentucky,
built between 1839 and 1841, stands to the east of the
community's Meetinghouse. Here, visitors from other Shaker
villages as well as "the World" dined, lodged, and did
business.

Trustees' Office, 1839-41, Pleasant Hill, Kentucky, from the west.

At Work

Every morning, a stream of communal family members left the dwelling like commuters on foot to disperse to their workshops, which made up the vast majority of buildings in any settlement. The division of the Shaker world into men's and women's spaces extended beyond the halls of the dwelling to all the work buildings.

The Shakers regarded women's and men's work as different but of equal worth. In spite of their acceptance of the traditional division of labor, in which Sisters did the cooking, cleaning, and textile work, while Brothers took care of the farming and heavy trades, the Shakers were actually much more egalitarian in their approach to work than their American contemporaries in the World. Women and men held equal positions of power

to the highest levels, women worked at trades that made income to help support the communal family, and men provided all the child care for the boys raised in the Society. In the big picture, the work roles of Shaker women and men were much more alike than different in terms of overall responsibility, differing mostly in the specific tasks.

One of the Shakers' principal reasons for adhering to the traditional work roles was their special interest in keeping men and women separate while living in the same community. As one Elder explained it, a Shaker Sister could not be a blacksmith because her companions would be men, and that was contrary to the Shaker way. For the same reason, a Shaker Brother could not work as a cook.

Although men and women were officially restricted from entering each others' work areas except with a same-sex partner, in real life Brothers and Sisters helped each other out when it was practical at tasks including herb work, apple gathering, soap making, and so on. Brethren were assigned to help the Sisters in the Wash House with lifting

heavy wet laundry, tending the fires, and running the machinery. Men also tended the fires and ran the machinery. Certain absolutely reliable Brothers, mostly men of advanced age and respectability, were designated drivers for groups of Sisters on the road on business or for visiting.

There were considerable advantages in the Shakers' communal economy. For one thing, members pooled resources and skills, making it possible for the communal family to support specialists in a variety of trades from butchering and tanning to shoemaking, dyeing, and tailoring.

Individual members were free to focus fully on the tasks at hand and were encouraged to devote their whole spirit to fulfilling their responsibilities faithfully and well for the love of God and each other. In their work, many Shakers seem to have found a special outlet for their gifts and personalities as individuals. For people for whom conformity in externals was so highly enforced—everyone had to dress alike, dance alike, rise, dine, and retire at the same hour, and so on—doing a particular task well was one of many ways to let one's own light shine. A Shaker could legitimately be recognized in his or her own communal family (and beyond, in the Shaker Society and even "the World") as a "good blue-dyer" or a "skilled woodworker."

Individual artisans did not have to concern themselves with either ongoing household chores like cooking and laundry or with the business of buying supplies and marketing their finished products. The business agents, Sisters and Brothers who served in the Office as Trustees, took care of the financial and commercial arrangements. The communal family's income, managed in most cases skillfully by the characteristically shrewd Office Brothers and Sisters, was in turn invested in the best, most modern equipment on the market to eliminate unnecessarily hard manual labor whenever possible. Another advantage was an increase in production. In the nineteenth century, Shaker communities were esteemed for their use of water and steam power; in the early twentieth century, the most active of the surviving communities converted early to electricity.

Much has been made by modern observers of the Shakers' association of work with worship. In fact, the Shakers themselves in the nineteenth century frequently quoted their founder Mother Ann Lee's words, both in the Society's official publications and in their own personal records and communications: "Put your hands to work and your hearts to God, and a blessing will attend you." Also: "Do all your work as though you had a thousand years to live, and as you would if you knew you must die tomorrow."

The association of work with an awareness of and reverence for a supreme being more powerful and knowledgeable than humans is, of course, perhaps one of the most ancient hallmarks of humankind. The Shakers believed that God, the source of all, was the provider of innate abilities as well as the capacity to learn more skills. If you improve in one talent, they said, God will give you more.

To this end, versatility was prized in Shaker life. Members were ordinarily expected to practice a half dozen trades with skill. The Shakers' system of rotating jobs promoted both spiritual growth for individuals and an assurance that the communal family would continue to function smoothly in the event that a particularly valuable or necessary craftsman died, moved to another communal family or village, or left the Society.

There was wisdom, as well, in encouraging members to continually learn new skills. The daily and yearly routine of Shaker life was quiet and relatively uneventful. The opportunity to move into a new workshop and master a new trade helped prevent boredom. While the Shakers found it practical and reasonable to place people where their greatest aptitude lay, the Society did not encourage any one member to believe that he or she "owned" a particular trade. At times, it seems clear that a member was transferred to another area of responsibility to free him or her from the feeling that he or she was indispensable, for the sake of promoting spiritual humility. Sometimes, too, the leaders deemed it wise to separate members who had become too close in the course of sharing work, because anything that fostered more private bonds at the expense of the communal good was regarded as undesirable for the sake of the community as a whole.

The Shakers took pains to design their homes so that they would not require more time than necessary to keep spotlessly clean. At Hancock, Massachusetts, the Church Family Sisters asked for and received the installation of a tin funnel and pipe that carried smoky fumes from an oil lamp directly to the chimney flue. They probably got the idea from another communal family of Shakers at nearby New Lebanon, New York, who seem to have innovated these "tin lilies" in the mid-nineteenth century. The funnel kept the smoke from blackening the ceiling and provided a good strong draft to make the flame burn brighter.

The peg rail, universal in Shaker interiors, provided convenient storage for chairs when the Sisters swept the floors. Hanging the chairs upside down kept the top of the seats from fading or gathering dust. These chairs hang near the elliptical arch on the second floor of the Church Family Dwelling, 1830-31, at Hancock, Massachusetts. The characteristic lightness of Shaker furnishings, which made housecleaning easier, was almost certainly a result of the Sisters' suggestions to the Brothers who built furniture.

162

A squadron of Sisters mustered daily to keep the large communal dwelling spotless. They liked to quote their founder, Mother Ann Lee, who was reported by those who knew her to have said, "There is no dirt in heaven," and "Good spirits will not live where there is dirt."

The Centre Family Sisters at South Union, Kentucky, were probably the brains behind the banister design in their dwelling, built from 1822 to 1833 under the direction of principal carpenter Brother Robert Johns. Raising the spindles made it much more convenient to mop or wash the floor.

Sisters took turns at kitchen duty, generally serving for four weeks at a time in a scheduled rotation. The Centre Family Sisters at Pleasant Hill, Kentucky, had kitchens on the first floor and in the cellar of their dwelling, begun in 1824 and finished in 1834. The room with the fireplace also has a brick beehive oven for the large weekly baking.

right
The peg rail in Shaker rooms was a great convenience for the Sisters who cleaned the communal family dwelling and for all male and female residents.

In the 1830-31 Church Family Dwelling at Hancock, Massachusetts, the builders threaded the base of each peg so it could not easily pull out as the wood dried and shrank a bit with the passage of time. The rail itself is built into the wall's construction, not merely tacked atop the plaster.

In some Shaker buildings, the peg rail strip simply serves as a neat cover for the construction underneath. In these cases, the threaded pegs twist all the way into the wooden ground, or base, built into the wall, and hold the peg rail strip in place.

The kitchen in the Church Family Dwelling, built at Hancock, Massachusetts, from 1830 to 1831, was designed to feed a communal family of nearly a hundred with efficiency. A rotating team of "kitchen Sisters" worked with state-of-the-art equipment in a room that was characteristically light, airy, and located on the basement level.

The lead builder and designer, Elder William Deming, was proud of the new accommodations: "The cook room is very convenient; we have excellent water from a never failing spring that is conveyed into the cook room in three different places and two places in the second loft [story]. There is [sic] two excellent ovens made on an improved plan which will bake four different settings at one heating. Also the arch kettles are on a new plan of my own invention, and which proves to be the best ever seen about here."

This view shows the two ovens with built-in arch kettles used for steaming, boiling, or stewing large quantities. In contrast to their neighbors in "the World," who still stooped over hearths to cook until the cookstove became more common by the 1850s, Shaker women worked at convenient, comfortable waist height. The floor was designed for both the safety and comfort of the women who worked here, combining fireproof marble near the wood-fired equipment, with wood, easier on the legs, in the work areas.

The smaller of the two ovens in the kitchen of the Church Family Dwelling, 1830-31, at Hancock, Massachusetts, was designed along improved plans published by inventor Count Rumford of New Hampshire and Europe in the 1820s. Behind the iron door are narrow shelves for baking pies.

First-floor fireplace, Smoke and Milk House, South Union, Kentucky.

left

The oven in the kitchen of the Church Family Dwelling, 1830-31, at Hancock, Massachusetts, like Shaker kitchen equipment in general, was designed and built on an institutional scale. Shaker Sisters prepared three meals a day for nearly a hundred members of their communal family in this room. Baking was akin to managing a commercial bakery. About once a week, Sisters rose early to build a fire in the oven, then raked out the coals and ashes. Huge batches of bread, cakes, biscuits, crackers, puddings, and baked beans went sequentially into the oven, where the heat retained in the bricks did the baking.

The 1835 Smoke and Milk House behind the Centre Family
Dwelling at South Union, Kentucky, was shared by the Sisters
and Brothers. The women did dairy work on one side and the
men tended the production of smoked hams on the other.

In 1894, the Church Family at Hancock, Massachusetts, built a new Ice House to accommodate two hundred tons of ice harvested from a nearby pond. The building served as a giant icebox or cooler. Triple doors, triple glazing in the windows, and packing the large frozen blocks in sawdust helped to keep the ice from melting before the end of the summer. The largest wall faces north to help cool the building.

The builders placed the Ice House on a hillside where natural underground coolness helped to preserve the ice stored in the right side of the structure. It is as close to the dwelling as possible, given the lay of the land, for the convenience of the cooks.

left

Elder William Deming, the principal designer and builder of the Church Family Dwelling, 1830-31, at Hancock, Massachusetts, explained that the purpose of the Shakers' characteristic built-in storage was twofold, saving space and facilitating cleanliness: "The drawers are faced with butternut and handsomely stained—they take up but little room, and are not to be cleaned under."

For most of Shaker history, rooms were heated with small, plain, cast-iron woodburning stoves. The Sisters swept away the inevitable wood ash daily in obedience to their founder Mother Ann Lee's instruction to clean their rooms well, so that the visible world would properly reflect inner spiritual purity.

above

Like hospitals and medical examining rooms, Shaker interiors were typically unadorned and stripped of furnishings to make cleaning as efficient as possible. The Sisters swept and dusted the dwelling's plaster walls and plain pine floors daily. In spring and fall, major housecleaning usually included a new coat of whitewash on the plaster walls and removal of the narrow woven rag carpets for washing or beating.

The Sisters' Dairy and Weave Shop built by the Church Family at Hancock, Massachusetts, in the 1790s, was doubled in size after 1820 when a second level was added. The bottom floor housed a profitable dairy operation, and the upstairs rooms were used for weaving and textile work.

left

Shaker men and women cooperated in designing and building in ways that eliminated unnecessary work. Wrought-iron foot scrapers at the entrances made it possible to leave most mud outside. This is the back door of the 1792 Meetinghouse at Canterbury, New Hampshire.

The Church Family at Canterbury, New Hampshire, built their first Laundry as part of the Spin Shop in 1795. By 1813 they had a "clothes drying house." They continued to modernize the equipment and facilities well into the twentieth century.

These slate sinks were added in 1902. The trap doors in the floor provide access to the Laundry's water supply, a cistern, and drainage system.

right

Shaker communal families customarily built separate work buildings, usually called shops or workshops, for the Sisters and Brothers.

The women in the East Family at Pleasant Hill, Kentucky, went to work Monday through Saturday in the Sisters' Shop, built around 1855 to replace an earlier log/frame workshop. Workrooms were equipped for a variety of enterprises including sewing, spinning, weaving, basket making, bonnet making, and the production of silk kerchiefs.

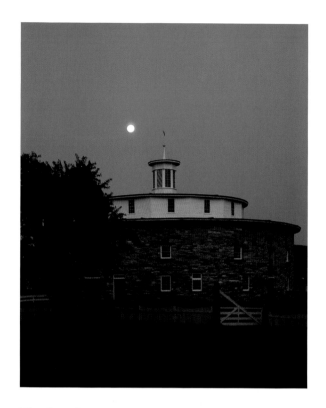

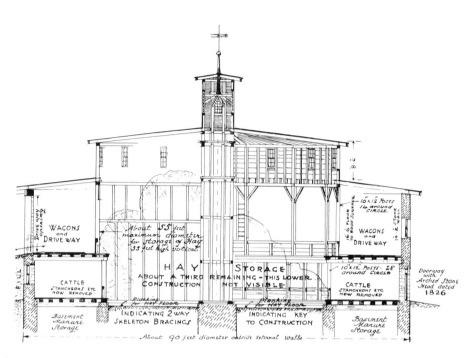

The dairy barn at Hancock, Massachusetts, is the only Shaker round barn. The three-story barn, a hundred feet across, has attracted visitors from the time it was built in 1826. Like other examples of Shaker technology, it represented state-of-the-art design and construction. Each floor—for wagons, cattle, and manure—could be reached from ground level by ramps. The unique circular design let farmers feed by simply forking hay a few feet from the huge central haymow to the stalls on the barn's perimeter.

The barn, which was widely published in nineteenth-century farm journals, was a landmark famous throughout the United States.

The central ventilator shaft in the Round Stone Barn, built in 1826 and rebuilt in 1864 by the Church Family at Hancock, Massachusetts, was designed to help prevent fire from spontaneous combustion in wet hay and to vent fumes from the manure cellar below the haymow floor, shown.

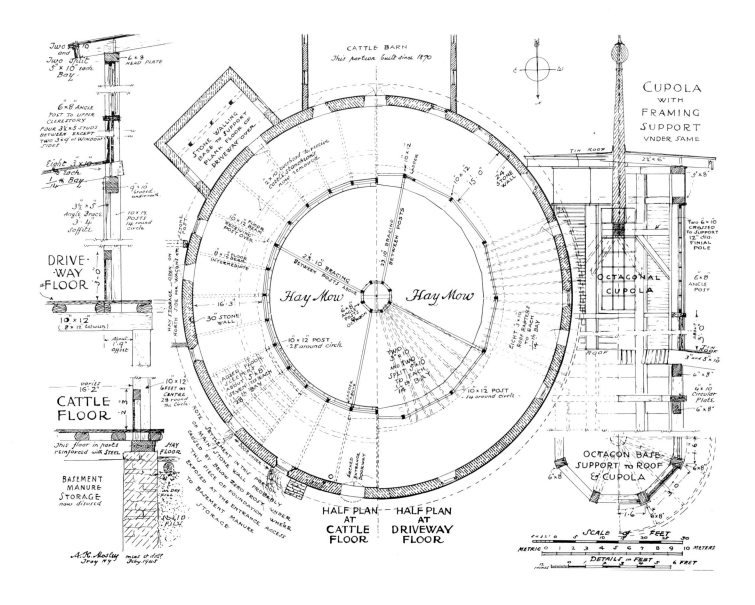

CATTLE BARN
This portion built since 1870

CUPOLA
WITH
FRAMING
SUPPORT
UNDER SAME

Hay Mow   Hay Mow

HALF PLAN
AT
CATTLE
FLOOR

HALF PLAN
AT
DRIVEWAY
FLOOR

DRIVE-WAY
FLOOR

CATTLE
FLOOR

BASEMENT
MANURE
STORAGE
now disused

OCTAGONAL
CUPOLA

OCTAGON BASE
SUPPORT TO ROOF
& CUPOLA

SCALE OF FEET

DETAILS IN FEET

This view is from the wagon level on the second floor. Each of the barn's three levels is accessible from the ground outside by means of an earthen ramp. Up to a dozen hay wagons at a time drove one way through and around and out the barn on this level. Shaker farmers pitched hay down into the huge haymow that took up most of the barn's space.

On the first floor, about sixty dairy cows were tied to stanchions for milking with their heads pointing to the center of the barn. The farmers walked between the stanchions and the haymow, efficiently forking hay across the walkway at feeding time.

The barn, which was fully restored in 1968, retains many of its original chestnut timbers.

The door on the second-floor wagon level of the Round Stone Barn at Hancock, Massachusetts, is not an exit but a convenient opening for tossing items down to the outside.

preceding page
After a fire in 1864 damaged the remarkable Round Stone Barn at Hancock, Massachusetts, constructed in 1826, the builders finished it again, this time making improvements. They raised the roofline to accommodate a clerestory level with windows to make the barn lighter and changed the shape of the roof from a shallow cone to a nearly flat surface.

The rafters were carefully designed and constructed to provide maximum support for the new roof. Each rafter is tapered, widening from its narrowest point where it joins the central ventilator shaft. Every other rafter has a "split end" that flares out to more fully support the edge of the roof where it meets the clerestory wall.

right
In 1838, the Church Family Shakers at Mount Lebanon, New York, built a large tannery to better accommodate their leather-working business, one of their primary money-making trades. Like most work buildings set away from the main road, it was painted a dark color.

From left to right, work buildings built by the Church Family at Canterbury, New Hampshire, include: the Schoolhouse, built in 1823 and raised to two stories in 1862; a long, low Cart Shed; the dark red Garage with its tower for drying fire hoses, built around 1908; a small shop originally used for pressing herbs; the Brethren's Shop, 1824, containing work areas for doctors, shoemakers, joiners, and farmers; and a Carriage House and workshop with a room for processing garden seeds and storage areas for wood and grain.

All of the buildings were Brothers' work buildings with the exception of the Schoolhouse.

One of the first buildings erected by the Church Family at Hancock, Massachusetts, was a combination Laundry and Machine Shop begun in the 1790s. It was unusual for women and men to work under one roof, but in this case, the building took advantage of a fine source of water power up the hill to the north, brought across the main road through the communal family's settlement by means of an underground aqueduct. The east half, shown, housed the machine shop, the Brothers' side of the building. In the west half, the Sisters washed, ironed, and dried clothes and household linens.

Laundry and Machine Shop, and Round Stone Barn, Hancock, Massachusetts.

In 1823 the Shakers in Canterbury, New Hampshire, built a one-room schoolhouse where the children who were cared for by the society could be taught. When the community eventually decided it needed a larger school, the entire building was raised and a lower room was added beneath, along with a woodshed, cloakroom, and three-hole privy.

Women and men spent equal time at work in the schoolhouse teaching the children cared for by the communal family, alternating according to season. In general, Sisters taught the girls in summer, when the boys and men were haying; Brothers taught the boys in winter, when girls helped with spinning and other work on the "Sisters' side." By the late nineteenth century, Shaker women taught both girls and boys.

The Canterbury Shakers were particularly noted for their interest in education and invested significantly in textbooks, supplies, and equipment, especially after about 1850. The blackboards are made of frosted glass painted black on the reverse. The teacher's desk, which was purchased, remains on the raised platform designed for it. The stovepipe travels the length of the room to help warm students sitting at a distance from the stove itself.

Large cast-iron fly wheels on a shaft remaining in the cellar of the North Family's Wash House at Mount Lebanon, New York, once helped operate commercial-size water-powered machines for laundering.

A trio of windows stretches daylight into the stairwell and drying room of the North Family Wash House at Mount Lebanon, New York.

ABCDEFGHIJKLMNOPQRSTUVWXYz
abcdefghijklmnopqrstuvwxyz &1234567890.

ABCDEFGHIJKLMNOP2RSTUVWXYZ
abcdefghijklmnopqrstuvwxyz&; :.:.?!0 October 31st 1825

left

Top of stairs, Schoolhouse, 1823-1862,
Church Family, Canterbury, New Hampshire.

A long alphabet board, dated 1825, helped show young Shaker scholars how to form block and script letters in the Schoolhouse at New Lebanon, New York.

In the 1860s, the North Family Shakers at Mount Lebanon, New York, converted the Wood House, built around 1854, to a laundry. Within a decade it featured water-powered washing equipment as well as facilities for drying and ironing.

The pentises, or pent roofs over the doors, made it easier for workers to stay dry while locking or unlocking when it rained. Part of the Lowland European building tradition, the pentise and sidelights reflect the influence on the Shakers of the Dutch-Americans who settled this part of New York.

By the late nineteenth century, the North Family Shakers had added convenient drying racks to their Wash House so that the Sisters could readily do the laundry for their large communal family whether it rained or was clear.

The Church Family Shakers at Canterbury, New Hampshire, installed a steam-drying room in their Laundry in 1854. In 1862, they remodeled the room with its similar sliding racks. Sharing ideas that worked was typical of the networking advantage enjoyed by the Shaker Society, which sought to foster cooperation rather than competition among its members.

above

Steps of the Sisters' Dairy and Weave Shop, circa 1795-1820, Hancock, Massachusetts.

In Between

Within the Shaker realm, the placement of the settlement in relation to "the World" outside was a primary concern of the first converts. After 1787, when the prototype community at New Lebanon, New York, showed that a Society-wide change to communal living apart from the World was both spiritually desirable and practical, the faithful in other enclaves in New England began to consider where to plant their own settlements.

Missionaries were sent from the Ministry at New Lebanon to the areas where an interest in the Shaker gospel existed. At this time, before they had special places for worship, the Shakers in those areas met in houses. The sites grew up as neighborhoods. Shakers purchased adjacent lands for their protection. If there was a large enough population, a

community was eventually gathered into order. Ideally, the site had good and ample farmland, water sources, woodlots, and a proper distance from the World—not too close, to avoid interference and influence from outsiders, but not too far, so they could travel to market to buy and sell as needed. The location selected was characteristically a farm already owned by a family whose members numbered among the converted.

With the establishment of the heart of the settlement in what was called the Church Family in New York and New England, and the Centre Family in Ohio and Kentucky (the English spelling was retained throughout the nineteenth century), the placement of the meetinghouse was generally the first order of business. The siting and building of the meetinghouse sometimes preceded the physical gathering of the communal family by a year or so, and its placement varied according to the choice of the particular community.

Typically, a flurry of building in the first decade or two of the community's existence produced a fine crop of new buildings clustered around the meetinghouse, with income-producing workshops usually taking precedence over larger, more comfortable

dwellings. When their resources permitted, the communal families designed and built more spacious dwellings. Since the Shakers deliberately tried to refrain from entering into debt to the World, the communal families usually waited until they could build what they needed for cash.

Within a few years of the establishment of the Church or Centre Family in any community, the growth of membership and the need for an interim "halfway house" experience led to the creation of a separate settlement, perhaps a half-mile or mile from the Church Family, as a Novitiate or "gathering" order. Here, newcomers and would-be Shakers were given the opportunity to try Shaker life before seriously considering the formal step of joining the Senior Order. The arrangement proved beneficial to both potential converts and the Society.

Within a few more years, a village typically needed additional expansion due to growth of membership. By the early 1800s, most had added Junior Orders and second locations of Senior and sometimes Novitiate Orders, typically clustered like satellites around the Church or Centre Family, within a distance of a quarter mile to a mile or two. Each additional communal family chose its location based on factors similar to those used by the original Church or Centre Family, characteristically settling on an adjacent farm owned by another converting household. By the mid-nineteenth century, Shaker villages included two to as many as eight separate communal families. Ordinarily, members of any one communal family were not allowed to visit another communal family without reason and permission from their leaders. In the 1840s, a member of a lower order at Enfield, New Hampshire, recalled the longing with which he gazed at the buildings of the highly revered Church Family, home of the Senior Order of Shakers, and how much he wished to be allowed to live there. (He was eventually transferred to the Senior Order but left after fifteen years, disillusioned finally with his experience there.)

Within any one settlement, the communal family generally had enough land and freedom to place buildings (and the spaces between them) where they were most useful—mills on streams, sawmills near woodlots, fields on good flat bottomland, pastures for sheep on hillsides, and so on. The Shakers' economic base in agriculture meant that buildings were customarily sited on land that wasn't first choice for planting or pasturing. Workshops for indoor trades seem to have been generally placed near the dwelling for the convenience of the members. The office and store was typically located on the main public road through the village wherever most passersby entered. At Hancock, Massachusetts, for example, since most travelers came from the town of Pittsfield five miles to the east, the Church Family built the office and store on the east side of their property.

Between buildings in any one communal family, fences and walks served, like links in a chain, to both unite and separate what they joined. Outsiders consistently commented on the neatness and good maintenance of Shaker fences. Visitors from the World also noted that most Shaker stone walks were noticeably narrow, forcing those who used them to walk single file rather than side by side. Shaker rule books specified that members were to stay on the prescribed straight and narrow path—evidently literally as well as metaphorically!

The blurring in the Shaker mind of the line between "heaven" and "earth," or as we might say, between the realms of idea or energy and matter, or as the nineteenth-century Shakers were more apt to say, between the "spiritual world" and the "natural world," was similarly evident in other manifestations of the Shakers' created environment in the material sphere. According to the spoken, written, and drawn messages from that other reality of the spirit world received and recorded by "instruments," or mediums, throughout Shaker history, the villages on earth took their shape from patterns in heaven. Shaker-style furniture and clothing appears in some representations of heaven in the "gift drawings" made in the mid-nineteenth century. The appearance of a Shaker settlement, from the unadorned, serviceable buildings to their particular spacing, was considered by members of the Shaker Society to have been divinely inspired.

North Family buildings from the Church Family,
Mount Lebanon, New York

View of the Centre Family Dwelling, 1824-24, from the
buildings of the East Family, Pleasant Hill, Kentucky.

A stone wall separates the fields and woodlots of the Church Family at Hancock, Massachusetts, from "the World's" main road through the property. To the north is Mount Sinai, the Hancock Shakers' sacred mountain, where the communal families marched to an outdoor worship area on special occasions in the 1840s.

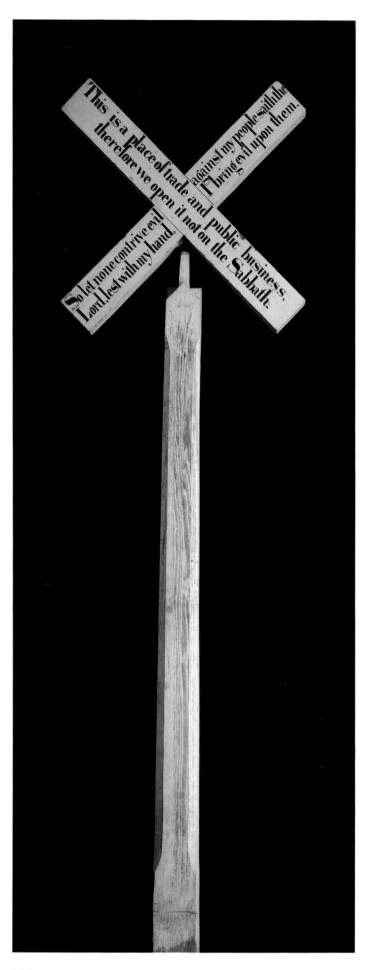

In 1842, the Shaker Society headquartered at New Lebanon, New York, decided to close worship meetings to visitors from "the World" for an unspecified period of time. They erected a post in front of the 1824 barrel-roofed meetinghouse and every Sunday mounted a cross-shaped notice to visitors, politely but firmly requesting them to turn back and not attempt to enter.

This similar cross-shaped sign was posted on Sundays in front of the Office and Store, where visitors were accustomed to purchasing mementoes of their visit to the Shaker village.

right
The Church Family Shakers at Canterbury, New Hampshire, built massive granite fieldstone walls. This section, southwest of the Meetinghouse, has the largest stones, some up to a yard across.

A simple white picket fence built in 1839 separates the Meetinghouse, 1794, and the 1839 Ministry's Shop at Sabbathday Lake, Maine, from "the World" passing through the village on the main road through the center of the Church Family. Today, that road—Maine Route 26—is a busy highway that sends tractor-trailers, Canadian tourists, skiers, and the occasional mass pilgrimage to a Grateful Dead concert roaring through the quiet settlement.

208

This view shows the risers installed to make visitors from "the World" welcome, comfortable, and properly removed from the members of the Shaker communal family. The double peg rail served as a coat and hat rack.

This view of the Meetinghouse at Sabbathday Lake, Maine, built in 1794, shows the hillside apple orchard behind and the distinctive shingled water tower built in 1903 as part of the fire safety system in the village. It is currently used for spraying in the apple orchard as well as for watering the herb and vegetable gardens.

left

From a doorway in the ell of their 1839 Ministry's Shop at Sabbathday Lake, Maine, the Ministry Eldresses and Elders could see the 1794 Meetinghouse, where they lived in the upper floors until the separate residence and workshop was built for them. This view was taken from the ell erected in 1875. The ell on the Meetinghouse dates from 1839.

right

A second-floor door on the wagon level of the Round Stone Barn built by the Church Family at Hancock, Massachusetts, opens to a view of the Sisters' Shop, which faces the Brothers' Shop. Both workshops date from the late 1790s. The Sisters' dairy rooms on the first floor of their shop were conveniently near the cows in the barn. The Hancock Church Family Shakers were well known for the quality of their butter and cheese.

Shakers sat on these built-in benches along the walls of the
1794 Meetinghouse at Sabbathday Lake, Maine, as well as on a
row of backless benches in front of them.

The Smoke and Milk House, built around 1835 (right), and the Wash House, 1854 (center), were located conveniently near the Centre Family Dwelling (left) at South Union, Kentucky. The Sisters did not have to carry laundry, or milk, cheese, and butter very far to the Dwelling's kitchen and retiring rooms.

following page
The work buildings used by members of any one Shaker living group clustered around the dwelling, the great heart of the communal family.

At Pleasant Hill, Kentucky, the East Family Sisters' Shop, built in 1855, adjoins the East Family Dwelling, built in 1817.

Church Family Buildings, Hancock, Massachusetts,
including white Trustees' Office and Store, 1813-1895, at far left
in background; red frame Tan House, 1835; large stucco barn,
1910; and Round Stone Barn, 1826-64.

View through Schoolhouse window, Church
Family, Canterbury, New Hampshire, showing Cart Shed; dark
red Garage, circa 1908; Creamery, 1905; and the Carpenter
Shop, 1806.

Church Family buildings, Canterbury, New Hampshire,
from the east: Church Family Dwelling, 1793-1837
(center); Sisters' Shop, 1816 (left); North Shop, 1842 (right);
Laundry, 1816 (far right); Creamery, 1905 (far background)

above

Stone walk looking west from south side of
Church Family Dwelling to east side of Laundry and Machine
Shop, Hancock, Massachusetts.

left

Schoolhouse, 1823-62, and Horse Barn, 1819,
Church Family, Canterbury, New Hampshire.

Elder Micajah Tucker of Canterbury, New Hampshire, cut more than a mile of granite walks for the Church Family.

It was not the custom in the nineteenth century for either "the World" or the Shakers to mow their dooryards often or at all. In most villages, Shakers kept their feet dry on neat stone walks. The paths were usually sufficiently narrow to discourage two members from walking too companionably abreast.

This limestone walk at Pleasant Hill, Kentucky, angles from the Centre Family Dwelling to the Water House, 1833, and the smaller Brethren's Bath House, built in 1860 as a place where the men could bathe. Sisters and boys and girls had separate bath houses.

Front steps, Church Family Office, 1840s, Harvard, Massachusetts.

left
View from front door of Church Family Office.

The gate post of a rock fence leading to the North Lot Dwelling at Pleasant Hill, Kentucky, is unusually finely finished, its surfaces dressed with "drove work," or shallow chiseled grooves, that radiate outward from the center of the half-round at the top.

Some Shaker communal families built wagon mounts to make it easier to climb into wagons or carriages. These exceptionally well-made freestanding stone and wrought-iron steps, from the community at Harvard, Massachusetts, are now at the Fruitlands Museums in the same town.

left

The Meetinghouse at Canterbury, New Hampshire, framed in 1792 under the direction of Brother Moses Johnson, sent from New Lebanon, New York, shows how far the Dutch-American architectural influence spread through the Shaker world. The particular configuration of two full windows as sidelights separated from the door was a common building tradition in Dutch New York—familiar to the first settlements of Shakers in Watervliet and New Lebanon—that the Shaker Society carried into New England.

In 1841, a member of the Church Family Shakers at New Lebanon, New York, was inspired to devise a pattern for the new meetinghouse fence. In the next year, the shape was copied in other Shaker villages.

At Canterbury, New Hampshire, the wooden pickets were set aboveground on neatly cut granite posts, preventing rot and virtually eliminating the need for repair or replacement.

Stone wall, Mount Lebanon, New York.

A rock fence near the East Family buildings at Pleasant Hill, Kentucky, has neatly built steps for the farmers' convenience in crossing.

Short stone post at gaps in the rail fence in front of the Meetinghouse in the Church Family at Harvard, Massachusetts, admit people—but not cows or horses—to the stone walks. The arrangement was a permanent and labor-saving alternative to gates, which always require ongoing maintenance and repair.

Twilight into Dawn
The Loss and Renewed Life of Shaker Buildings

By the 1840s, Shakers in several communities were beginning to express concern about a reduction in their numbers of converts. By 1900, the population was lower than it had been since the Society's early years in America, although the spirit of the people who continued to live, work, and pray in Shaker villages was in many cases undiminished. In an effort to attract new members, progressive young and middle-aged leaders led a campaign to modernize their image without sacrificing the bedrock principles on which

the Society was founded. Instead of eliminating the requirement of celibacy, for example, the Society chose instead to make allowances for the comfort and convenience of members and potential converts by permitting a variety of formerly forbidden, innocent pleasures, including musical instruments, harmony in sacred song, pets, flower gardens, more outings, more worldly books and magazines, and a bit of trim on clothing, furniture, and buildings.

Building continued, albeit at a more moderate pace. In 1910, the Church Family at Hancock, Massachusetts, invested in a huge new barn for the dairy operation (by this time, run almost entirely by hired workers because the number of Brothers had declined). Other communities that were able and so inclined added modern dairy buildings, electrical generating plants, and small, airy, screened summer houses for the convenience, comfort, and pleasure of the members.

232

In time, however, as the number of Shaker people diminished, communal families one by one began to close their doors, dismantle their buildings, and consolidate their members in other, larger settlements. By the turn of the twentieth century, some entire communities had dissolved, their remaining members then moving to other, more thriving villages. As the numbers dropped, the Shaker Society chose to dismantle or sell most of the buildings that were no longer in use to reduce property taxes and to avoid

maintaining vacant buildings. Some buildings were sold to outsiders in "the World," where they were converted into residences and entered a new kind of service. Others were razed and the parts recycled or sold, again, in the Shaker mind, to make thrifty use of the resources God provided.

By 1959, three of the original nineteen Shaker communities remained as living homes for Shaker people. By that time, other Shaker village sites had been sold to the World, where the properties entered various new phases of usefulness as county homes for the aged, schools, prisons, hospitals, and monasteries for other religious orders. The non-Shaker buyers frequently dismantled more buildings after the Shakers sold the land and departed.

In 1960, the community at Hancock, Massachusetts, was sold by the Shaker Society directly to the nonprofit organization that continues to maintain the property as a museum dedicated to presenting the Shaker way of life to visitors from America and around the world. This represented a giant step in the preservation of Shaker culture. Fine museum and archival collections had been formed with the cooperation of Shaker leaders since around 1900, and pioneer collector Clara Endicott Sears had in 1920 purchased and moved a small Shaker office to her museum grounds at Fruitlands, Massachusetts, but Hancock was the first site to be acquired with the cooperation of the Shaker Society for saving. At the same time, buildings in several of the communal families at Pleasant Hill, Kentucky, were acquired by another, separate nonprofit organization for preservation as a museum and conversion to modern lodging and dining facilities in the traditional Shaker style. (At Pleasant Hill, the buildings had been sold years earlier to non-Shakers, who had not made irreversible changes to the buildings' interiors or exteriors.)

Today, we are fortunate to have so many surviving examples of Shaker buildings. While much exists only in memory, written records, and photographs and measured drawings—in what the Shakers themselves might call the spirit world—the buildings that remain in the "natural" world or material world of stone, brick, and timber testify to the qualities valued in Shaker life.

While not every one was a masterpiece, the buildings as a whole give evidence of the care and skill of their makers. They seem to have been built to last for the millennium that the Shakers envisioned, sturdy and spacious enough to provide shelter and livelihood for a thousand generations of Shakers to come. They were made to suit the practical purposes of an eminently practical people, and if they presented a public image of deliberate simplicity and restraint, it was secondary to the primary purpose of putting God's resources into useful service.

Dining room doors, Church Family Dwelling, Hancock, Massachusetts.

The dry-laid fieldstone walls, at Pleasant Hill, Kentucky, called rock fences in that region, are like those built by hired Irish workers who brought their traditions and skills from across the Atlantic. The Shakers' fences looked like those of their neighbors in "the World" around, but the sheer size of their vast acreage meant that the Shakers had lots more miles of fence to build.

The Centre Family Shakers at South Union, who occupied
their dwelling for nearly a hundred years after it was
completed in 1833, made changes over time, even during the
decade of the building's construction. The fireplaces in the
retiring rooms, or sleeping rooms, were replaced with
woodstoves before the Family first moved in, but the original
wooden mantels remain. After 1900, the woodstoves were
themselves replaced with grates for burning coal. This is the
first-floor retiring room on the Sisters' side.

The built-in cupboard and case of drawers, similarly
modernized with white china pulls, is unusual for its subtle
trompe l'oeil effect—a narrow strip along the left edge and
the simple but bold cornice give the unit the appearance of a
freestanding piece.

In 1860, the railroad came through Shaker land at South
Union, Kentucky. Nine years later, recovering from the
economic assault of the Civil War on their pacifist community,
the South Union Shakers built a tavern as a commercial
venture to serve rail passengers.

The great white columns are brick finished to look like stone.
The numbers in the date 1869 are carved in relief and
painted.

View into 1875 ell, Ministry's Shop, 1839, Sabbathday Lake, Maine.

Built-in cupboard and drawers, looking into sink room
from Sisters' Workroom in Ministry's Shop, 1839, Sabbathday Lake, Maine.

In the later nineteenth and early twentieth century, Shakers in communities including Sabbathday Lake, Maine, and Canterbury, New Hampshire, painted much of their interior woodwork white for a fresh, more modern look. The drawer pulls and pegs in the peg rail in the Sisters' Workroom of the Ministry's Shop built at Sabbathday Lake in 1839 and extensively renovated in 1875 were left unpainted, probably for the practical reason that constant use would have worn the paint off. The effect, however, is pleasing to the eye.

The 1839 built-in cupboards and drawers in the Brothers' bedroom of the Ministry's Shop, built by the Church Family Shakers at Sabbathday Lake, Maine, were painted blue. The interiors retain their original yellow paint.

The use of single rather than double drawer pulls is a characteristic of built-in and freestanding case furniture in Shaker villages in Maine and New Hampshire. A drawer with a single central pull can be opened more conveniently by someone with an armful of this or that.

In 1875, the Church Family at Mount Lebanon, New York, lost their original frame dwelling and other buildings in a fire set by an arsonist. Although the communal family rebuilt a large dwelling, this time in brick, the community never really fully recovered from the emotional and economic loss caused by the fire. The destruction of the original home and its contents represents a loss of some of the finest work made by the Shakers, since the Church Family members at Mount Lebanon were regarded throughout the Society as models to be emulated, and their work as the pinnacle of perfection and achievement.

When the Shakers at Mount Lebanon, New York, built their marvelous new barrel-roofed meetinghouse in 1824, they moved the original 1785 meetinghouse to the north and subsequently used it as a schoolhouse and seed house. With major later changes, especially to the roofline, it is no longer recognizable as the prototype for the other gambrel-roofed meetinghouses framed by Brother Moses Johnson throughout the New England Shaker communities. The Mount Lebanon Shakers' tendency to move, rebuild, or raze buildings for practical reasons was characteristic of other Shaker communities.

As many as 140 years ago, the Mount Lebanon Shaker Village had lost most of its early architectural legacy. In 1858, Shaker scribe Brother Isaac Newton Youngs noted the loss or change of nearly all the buildings that he knew in his youth: "And by about the year 1850 there was not one building left standing as it was in 1805, or as late as 1810..."

At the turn of the twentieth century, having celebrated their centennial in 1890, the Church Family Shakers at Hancock, Massachusetts, were still building, in spite of their severe drop in numbers, especially among the Brothers. A new brick Ice House, built in 1894 "with modern improvements" to store two hundred tons of ice, was set on a hillside to take advantage of natural underground coolness. Behind, to the south, is the enormous stucco-covered timber-frame barn built in 1910.

The Shaker community at Hancock, Massachusetts, was the third earliest to gather, in 1790, and was one of the last three surviving villages when the property was put on the market in 1959. The extant Church Family buildings were sold in 1960 to a nonprofit museum organization, which began to restore and open the buildings.

Schoolyard fence, added in 1909, Church Family, Canterbury, New Hampshire.

Porch bracket, added in 1850 to Sisters' Shop, 1816, Church Family, Canterbury, New Hampshire.

In the late nineteenth and twentieth centuries, the Shaker Society relaxed its once rigid stance against ornament and accepted trim on buildings, furniture, and dress. However, Shaker buildings, although deliberately outmoded in terms of style for most of the nineteenth century, are understood best as a simplified, streamlined version of what "the World" was building at the same time in the same area of America. Ornament in Shaker life from the Victorian era is "fancy" only in comparison with the early-nineteenth-century plainness of country buildings in Shaker villages *and* the World. Details like this porch bracket on the Laundry at Canterbury, New Hampshire, added in the late nineteenth century, are restrained versions of what neighbors in the World around were building at the same time.

Turned urn on front porch added in 1917 to
Church Family Dwelling, Canterbury, New Hampshire,
with 1792 Meetinghouse in background.

The Church Family Shakers at Canterbury, New Hampshire,
were typically progressive and enthusiastic about assimilating
modern technology. In 1907 they bought their first automobile
and built this garage for it in 1908. The tower was used to dry
and store hoses for the communal family's fire engine. The
pressed metal siding was part of an effort to modernize the
community's appearance in hopes of attracting more converts.

In 1858 the North Family at Mount Lebanon, New York, a
gathering, or Novitiate, order where would-be converts tried
the Shaker life before formally joining, built a magnificent five-
story stone barn. At more than two hundred feet long, it was
thought to be the largest barn in the Northeast and possibly
all of America.

In 1972, this splendid barn burned in a fire attributed to
arson. Since then, the barn remains impressive even in ruins.

After the Church Family at Canterbury, New Hampshire, added an ell with a large meeting room to their Dwelling in 1837 they did not meet as often in the old 1792 Meetinghouse. In 1878, however, progressive young Elder Henry Clay Blinn freshened the Meetinghouse with a new coat of light blue paint over the dark blue from 1815.

The timber braces, neatly boxed with finished woodwork, are part of the structure that allows the first floor of the meetinghouse to be an open space uninterrupted by interior columns. This method of construction reveals the influence of the Dutch bent framing system in upstate New York, familiar to Shakers in New Lebanon, New York, where the prototype for Shaker meetinghouses was constructed in 1785.

The Church Family at Canterbury, New Hampshire, was relatively conservative. Instead of building a new dwelling in the mid-nineteenth century, like many other large communal families, they simply altered and added to their original 1793 Dwelling well into the twentieth century. The Canterbury community also moved and rehabbed buildings for different uses as the needs of the communal families changed. To the west of the Dwelling is what is now called the Enfield House, built originally by Canterbury's Second Family in 1794 as an office. In 1921, after Canterbury's sister village closed at Enfield, New Hampshire, the few remaining members moved to this building at Canterbury, which was moved in 1918 to this site in the Church Family for their comfort and convenience.

In the late nineteenth and early twentieth century, the Church Family Shakers at Canterbury, New Hampshire, updated their old Sisters' Shop, built in 1816, the Dwelling, and other work buildings with white paint on some of the interior woodwork.

The stone foundation is all that remains of an unidentified mill or workshop in the Shaker community at Tyringham, Massachusetts. In 1875, Tyringham was the first entire Shaker settlement to close completely, although communal families had previously ceased to exist one at a time in other villages.

In the second half of the twentieth century, preservationists began to renew many surviving Shaker buildings to something like their original neatness. Today many of these venerable structures combine the old and the new, like the paint on an upstairs door in the Smoke and Milk House, built around 1835 by the Centre Family at South Union, Kentucky. Since 1971, the site has been owned and operated as a non-profit museum organization called Shakertown at South Union, dedicated to the preservation of this part of Kentucky's Shaker heritage.

The historic Shaker Village at Pleasant Hill, Kentucky, employs master stonemasons for restoration work who practice the same skills and cut limestone from the same quarry that their Shaker predecessors used.

In 1972, the small group of elderly Shakers still living in the Church Family at Canterbury, New Hampshire, formed a nonprofit organization called Shaker Village to provide for the preservation of their village site and culture after their passing. Today, Canterbury Shaker Village devotes itself to this ongoing responsibility. In 1990, the Horse Barn (right) built in 1819, was extensively repaired and reshingled.

In the later nineteenth century, the Canterbury Shakers painted most of their buildings white. The large wagon doors have a painted panel where they meet, an unusual feature in this region although common on barns in upstate New York, settled by Dutch-Americans—perhaps a legacy of the Shakers' roots in that area when they settled in America.

In 1920, the remarkable Clara Endicott Sears moved the Shaker Office, built in 1794 in the Church Family at Harvard, Massachusetts, to the magnificent hillside site of her new Fruitlands Museums. Here, on the site of the original farm homestead called Fruitlands where Bronson Alcott (father of writer Louisa May) and others attempted and soon abandoned their own version of the communal life in 1843, she established museums to preserve the artifacts and interpret the culture of the Shakers and Native Americans, as well as exhibiting works by the Hudson River school of painters.

Miss Sears, who had earlier befriended members of the dwindling community at Harvard, which closed in 1918, acquired and saved one of the earliest and finest collections of Shaker material well in advance of most other pioneering scholars, collectors, historians, and enthusiasts.

The original Schoolhouse built around 1820-30 by the Church Family at Hancock, Massachusetts, was sold by the Shakers in the twentieth century and moved off the site for conversion to a private residence. After the property opened as a restored museum village in 1960, a restoration building team was able to measure the original to build this exact replica, complete with woodshed and privies for boys and girls. Neatly aligned with it along the main road through the village are the Horse Barn, 1850, and Ministry Shop, 1874.

The Meetinghouse now at Hancock, Massachusetts, is a remarkable architectural rehabilitation story. The original Hancock Meetinghouse, begun in 1786, was razed by the Shakers in 1938. After the village opened as a restoration in 1960, the museum organization was able to purchase a virtually identical Shaker meetinghouse—from a former Shaker village property sold for conversion to a prison—and moved it to the site of Hancock's original meetinghouse in 1962. This Meetinghouse was built by the Shakers in Shirley, Massachusetts, within a few years of construction of the Hancock Meetinghouse.

Hancock Shaker Village on a winter afternoon.

266

The round barn in high summer.

It seems fitting that we are able to present this book at this time. Nineteen ninety-four is the bicentennial celebration of the formal gathering of the Shaker community at Sabbathday Lake, Maine, although converts to the Shaker faith in that area had assembled to worship together for some years before the official move to communal life. At this time the sole remaining living group of Shaker people, the members anticipate the vital continuation of the Shaker faith and traditions into the twenty-first century and beyond. Like Shakers since the days of founder Mother Ann Lee more than two centuries ago, this communal family looks forward more than backward. When the Sabbathday Lake Shakers gather to worship in the 1794 meetinghouse, the spirit shown signifies the devotion that created and continues to sustain Shaker life.

Acknowledgments

This book took shape at the suggestion of Paul Rocheleau, who first proposed a photographic book on Shaker architecture in 1986, when he and I joined forced on *Shaker Design,* the catalog accompanying a major exhibition at the Whitney Museum of American Art and Corcoran Gallery of Art. I am grateful to have been asked to participate in this book.

In this project, my role has been more that of an editor and writer than scholar, since the information about the buildings has come directly from the people who work most closely with them, in the one remaining living Shaker community in Sabbathday Lake, Maine, and in the other former Shaker village sites, some of which are now maintained as museums and restorations. My contribution consists primarily of sharing knowledge about the social history of Shaker buildings and weaving the photographs and facts into a story. The text is a truly collaborative effort and could not have been written without the knowledge, insight, and generosity of the following individuals, who provided the information used in the captions for the buildings at the Shaker village sites in their care:

Leonard Brooks, Director, The Shaker Museum, and the United Society of Shakers, Sabbathday Lake, Maine

Tom Donnelly, Director, Mount Lebanon Shaker Village, New Lebanon, New York

Robert D. Farwell, Director, The Fruitlands Museums, Harvard, Massachusetts

Tommy C. Hines, Executive Director, Shakertown at South Union, Kentucky

John Harlow Ott, former Director, Hancock Shaker Village, Inc., Pittsfield, Massachusetts

Carolyn A. Smith, Director, and Michael O'Connor, Administrative Assistant, The Museum at Lower Shaker Village, Enfield, New Hampshire

Dr. Scott Swank, Executive Director, and Shery Hack, Curator of Buildings, Canterbury Shaker Village, Inc., Canterbury, New Hampshire

Jim Thomas, President and CEO, and Larrie Curry, Director of Collections, Shaker Village of Pleasant Hill, Harrodsburg, Kentucky

June Sprigg

In addition, we are deeply grateful to Don Carpentier, Director and Founder, Eastfield Village, East Nassau, New York, for his significant involvement in this project. Don read the text for corrections, added specific architectural information, shared his knowledge and collection of early American builders' tools, and greatly enriched the book's content in regard to eighteenth- and nineteenth-century American and Shaker building materials, tools, and techniques.

We are also grateful to the following individuals and organizations for their gracious assistance:

The Abode of the Message, New Lebanon, New York

Canterbury Shaker Village, New Hampshire: Karen Smith

Katherine D. Finkelpearl, Harvard, Massachusetts

Jerry Grant, former Assistant Director for Collections and Research, The Shaker Museum and Library, Old Chatham, New York, for information on Brother Richard Woodrow's hole-boring machine

Hancock Shaker Village, Massachusetts: Lawrence J. Yerdon, Director

Donald McDonald, New Lebanon, New York

Mount Lebanon Shaker Village, New York: Jenny Richards

Shaker Village of Pleasant Hill, Kentucky: Martha Sue Mayes, Cornell Powell, Lynn Reynolds, Vivian Yeast

Shakertown at South Union, Kentucky: James Grinter, Sharon Koomler, Mike Sisk